Reunion

the extraordinary story
of a messenger
of love & healing

Reunion

the extraordinary story
of a messenger
of love & healing

BY JESSICA EZELL

✴ STILLPOINT PUBLISHING

✳STILLPOINT PUBLISHING
Building a society that honors the Earth,
Humanity, and the Sacred in All Life
Copyright © 1996 by Jessica Ezell

This book was manufactured in the United States of America.
Cover Design by Kathryn Sky-Peck
Text Design by Heather Gendron
Cover Photo courtesy of Helaine Iris, Jeremey Youst, and "Cloud"

Published by Stillpoint Publishing, P.O. Box 640,
Meetinghouse Road, Walpole, NH 03608

ISBN: 1-883478-17-0

DEDICATION

This book is dedicated to the memory of my last and forever love, Zeke Ezell; my beloved angel, Daby; my first love, Benny L. Roberts; and to my father, Garvis N. Fleming, who taught me about forgiveness.

And to all of you who have had to say that last farewell to someone you deeply love—whose spirit, you know with certainty, walks beside you.

TABLE OF CONTENTS

ACKNOWLEDGMENTS

I wish to express my heartfelt gratitude for those who have believed in the story of Zeke and Daby and who encouraged me to write it.

To all of Zeke's children who supported me in this endeavor: Sherri Ezell, for her beautiful poem; Alvatti Lannom; Harley Ezell and his wife, Julie; special appreciation and gladness for my beautiful "Patty Ann," whose excitement and joy over this book helped spur my writing attempts and who spent many hours at her computer with the manuscript, and for her husband, Roger Williams, always helpful and supportive to both of us.

To my son, John Roberts, for allowing me to use his wonderful poetry and whose love and courage in the face of his own profound losses have given me immeasurable hope; to his wife, Laura; to my mother, Somar Fleming, and my sister, Dorian Rogers, who gave me continuing encouragement; to my loving and affirming friends and spiritual mentors, Ellison and Sharon (Bishka) Pusser, who were with me from the beginning; to my friend and working partner, Gini Medanich, herself a writer, who encouraged me when my energy for writing grew dim; to my longtime friend, Terry Burnett, for sharing with me her own painful losses and for always being there for me in so many ways; to Joy Richards, who walked with me in my deepest grief; to Bunny Morgan, my friend and guide, who never stopped calling to tell me that she cared.

And most of all, my deepest gratitude to Claire Gerus, my editor, who was first to affirm and validate my experience with Daby and who believed in the story and my ability to write it in book form before I had even begun.

FOREWORD

I was never certain that *To Dance with the White Dog* would be published.

Too personal, I believed.

Who would care about the death of my parents, even in the dress-up language of fiction?

And I was almost right.

New York publishers rejected the manuscript—all with kind, praising letters. A touching story, they wrote. They admitted to tears, to memories of their own parents or grandparents. It was a book they would *like* to publish, they confessed, yet it was also a book with risk.

What does one do with a story containing no violence and no sex, based on a Southern family that was not dysfunctional?

Thankfully, Peachtree Publishers, Ltd. of Atlanta, a regional publishing company, decided to take the risk.

The book was released in the fall of 1990. Soon after, the letters began arriving, letters telling of similar white dog (or white wolf, or white cat, or white dove) experiences.

Letters containing photographs. Letters with the simple words, "Thank You," written almost like a whisper.

A retired doctor called from Tennessee, telling me that he had been reading *To Dance with the White Dog* to a group of elderly ladies in a nursing home. It had taken a year to get through the book because the ladies would assume the roles, would interrupt to tell their own stories.

A woman in Minnesota canceled a flight to greet me at a book store because she had found healing in the story of the death of my parents.

A woman who worked in a funeral home told me at a gathering in Atlanta that she provided copies of my book to grieving families to help them understand the comfort of good memories.

After a speech in South Carolina, a young woman told me she had driven fifty miles to introduce someone to me— "The white dog," she said. She had the dog with her, in her truck. The dog had appeared to her shortly after the death of her father.

Such are the moments that make writers feel as though their work was not wasted, and I think I have known for years that someone would write again of the white dog.

That someone is Jessica Ezell. In *Reunion*, she tells a touching story of the death of her husband only five days after watching the Hallmark Hall of Fame presentation of *To Dance with the White Dog* on CBS Television. The movie, starring Hume Cronyn and the late Jessica Tandy, was another risk that proved a worthy gamble. In 1993, it was the top-rated motion picture on television.

I will not spoil Jessica Ezell's story with remarks that skip rocks across the pond of her own extraordinary adventure with Daby, the white dog that appeared to her after the unexpected death of her husband, Zeke. The story tells itself in a simple, honest, straightforward manner.

But I do want to say this: I believe in the white dog, and it does not matter to me if that dog has the look of a German shepherd or a malamute or a poodle. I believe the same stories of wolves and cats and birds, of turtles and gerbils and deer.

And I believe there are millions of people who also believe, or want to believe, and if that is true, then those people who are afraid of the risk in telling such stories are wrong about what people want to read, or to view.

After *Reunion* is published, the letters will begin arriving at Jessica Ezell's address.

I would like to be the first to write.

Dear Jessica,
Thank you.

—Terry Kay,
author, *To Dance with the White Dog*

PART 1

Jessica and Zeke

TO ZEKE

Somewhere beyond memory
I have known you
And loved you,
Was fated to meet with you
Again on some sun-washed shore
To finish our souls' work
Together.

I love you
For all the things you are
And you are
All the things I love.

JESSICA
From a love note
1-12-92

CHAPTER ONE

EMERGENCY

I HAVE A STORY TO TELL, an incredible, astonishing experience that, years later, still defies my ability to grasp its full impact. It is a story about being brushed by the Divine, about opening my eyes to the seemingly ordinary and discovering an enchanted world where the Divine truly lives in all Nature, all beings, and in the world around me. Sometimes the vividness of this world is fleeting, like the brilliant red and gold of a sunset. Sometimes it explodes upon me like a thousand suns indelibly imprinting their radiance on my soul.

This story is also about learning that one must be open, ready to see and embrace the gift, experience it fully in the here and now, savor it, and then release it when its time has passed.

Most of all, this is a story about the immense power of love.

I am telling this story simply to share its magic, to honor its impact on my life, and to pass on to others its message of hope and healing.

SATURDAY EVENING, DECEMBER 18, 1993

This is the night when the world will spin off its axis, careening crazily through time and space, changing my life forever. I've been at work for about an hour, having left my husband, Zeke, sprawled on the sofa, complaining mildly of a sinus headache. Always the nurse, I'd checked his blood pressure; then, relieved that it was normal, I'd brushed a kiss quickly across his lips and dashed out to begin my shift at Tennessee Christian Medical Center.

Once here, I'm swept up into the chaos of the Chemical Dependency Unit, where I work as a nurse. I'm just beginning to sort through the shambles of the preceding shift when someone yells, "Jessica, phone!" Olin, a good friend and neighbor, is on the line, his voice a bit too loud, too upbeat. He tells me he's with Zeke at our house.

"He's having chest pain. It's very severe," he tells me, his voice now betraying his fear.

"But is he . . . what does he look like?" I ask anxiously.

"Is he breathing O.K.?" My heart is pounding. I know that chest pain can signal an impending cardiac arrest.

"He's in really bad pain, and I've called an ambulance," Olin now reveals. Then he says, "Wait a minute. He wants to talk to you."

Zeke's voice, tense and fearful, booms loudly into the telephone. "Honey? Can you come to me? Can you come to me?"

Accustomed to his usually relaxed tone, I feel alarm and anxiety shoot twin arrows through me. *Stay calm*, I tell myself, and quickly assure him, "Yes, yes, of course I'll be there. I'm hanging up now to notify Staffing."

Replacing the phone on its hook, I sit frozen in my chair in front of my computer. I'd been frantically entering orders on a new patient, and another is waiting to be admitted. I'm also aware of several volatile situations that require my immediate attention. But my mind is reeling with an onslaught of images. *Zeke . . . chest pain. It can't be serious! Most likely it's gas or muscle spasms or some such thing.*

Tears begin to sting my eyelids. *We have really just begun. It is too soon to lose him.* I manage to stand. My working partner, Gini, catches my eye as she rushes by and stops abruptly.

"Jessica?"

"It's Zeke. He's on his way to St. Thomas Hospital in an ambulance. Chest pain. I'll need to leave right away."

Collapsing into my chair, I pick up the receiver to tell Staffing of my need to leave. Within minutes, my dear friend, Bishka, is standing before me, called from her unit to fill in until another nurse arrives. She and Gini stand together, mute, looking stricken. I move toward them as if in slow motion as sounds of the unit begin to fade. Looking into their eyes, reaching my arms out to them, I seem to be in a vortex where all things are known, and the past, present, and future are one. I know. They know. We all feel a terrible foreboding.

I don't want to leave them, to walk away and fall into the terrifying abyss of the unknown. Here I'm safe, temporarily, in their arms.

But the clamor and noise of the unit surround me once again, and I know I must leave the safety net of their love. "I'll call you as soon as I know anything," I promise my friends, reluctantly pulling away.

Soon I'm in my car, on my way to St. Thomas Hospital, my breathing shallow and fast, my hairs beginning to prickle on my neck, thoughts spinning, images of the past week flashing through my mind.

Sunday Night, December 12, 1993

I'm here at work, and Zeke has called me three times while recording a TV movie.

Gini hands me the phone receiver, laughing. "It's Zeke again, asking to speak to 'my darlin' Jessica.'"

"O.K., Sweetie, what now?" I smile. I can never be annoyed with Zeke. I'd take his calls anywhere, anytime. The sudden thrill I feel at the sound of his voice hasn't changed since our dating days.

"Oh, Honey, I'm so excited about this movie, I just can't wait for you to see it! The title is *To Dance with the White Dog,* and it's an incredible story." Zeke is bubbling over with excitement.

I can't resist a grin at his enthusiasm. But when I've hung up, I remark to Gini, "How odd. I've never known him to be so excited, so completely taken . . . with a movie."

MONDAY EVENING, DECEMBER 13, 1993

After dinner and before watching the movie, Zeke and I take our coffee and move out onto the deck in the waning light of the evening. The deck overlooks the river, with the shoreline only yards from the rear of the house. We often see wild ducks, geese, and deer along its banks. I love hearing the quacking of the ducks and watching them glide easily through the water.

This is our dream come true, this house by the river— not because it's fancy, but because Zeke and I both love the water. Zeke has always been a true "water man," made for it and at home on it. He knows everything there is to know about fishing, and he loves his old boat with its small trolling motor.

As we sip our coffee, I look at him, still in wonderment after two years of marriage. He's just turned sixty, and yet he seems so young, looks so handsome. I love his passion—about everything. A shock of dark brown hair falls over his forehead as he leans back in his deck chair and props a long leg up on the deck rail. Suddenly, he leans forward, looking down into the water.

"Look! See those two shining eyes moving down the center of the river?" I follow Zeke's finger and see a pair of glowing eyes rapidly slipping through the water at a constant speed, never wavering from side to side, in perfect harmony with the water.

"I'm grateful for my life as a man," Zeke says with a sigh, "but oh, to be a water creature, a sea creature completely at home in the water, at one with it."

Then, standing up, he holds out his hand and says, "Let's go watch *To Dance with the White Dog*."

We sit on the sofa and hold hands as the story softly wraps its ribbon of magic around us. Zeke had watched the movie earlier while recording it for me. Now, from time to time, he leans forward in anticipation, sometimes chuckling, sometimes rubbing at tears that fill his eyes, then looking at me through his fingers and laughing sheepishly.

The story revolves around a recently deceased wife whose spirit of eternal love is sent to the adored husband she has left behind. The messenger is a white dog that closely resembles a dog they had owned and loved earlier in their marriage. It is a beautiful and moving story, with excellent acting by Hume Cronyn and Jessica Tandy, themselves a devoted married couple off screen.

After the movie, Zeke surprises me by taking my hand in both of his, his eyes growing grave, his voice very serious. "Do you want me to come back to Earth to take care of you for a while, for one last goodbye . . . after I die?" he asks.

Taken aback, I pause for a moment. Then, seeing that he's serious, I reply, "Well, yes! But I wouldn't want you to feel Earthbound, and I'm sure that you'll be caught up in more exciting and adventurous things to do in the spirit world!"

He makes no reply, just looks at me and smiles.

I am now back in the present, racing toward the hospital. I've missed my exit on the downtown loop, and panic rises as I press my foot down hard on the gas pedal. The next exit is still several miles away.

"Oh, Zeke," I whisper. "Hang on, Darling." Suddenly, his face flashes before me, and I remember the first time I saw the man I'd love as I had never loved anyone before.

June 12, 1990

I've just accepted a nursing position at a local Alcohol and Drug Treatment Center, the very place where I stopped my own downward spiral ten years ago. It was here that I inexplicably turned one moment and looked into the unblinking eye of my own destiny, to be forever changed.

A tall, big-boned man with brown hair and brown eyes is walking toward me—the classic "big lug" with a crooked grin. Zeke is the night counselor and has just come into Medical, making his rounds. We sit chatting for a few minutes, talking easily together. His keen sense of humor has already intrigued me, and I'm curious to know more about him.

Suddenly, a former patient of his enters the room, someone who had gone home and continued his recovery. His healing shows on his face and in his demeanor. I'm still looking at Zeke when he first sees the man walk in, just before he springs to his feet and rushes toward him. Never before have I seen such a look on an adult's face. It radiates sheer love, sheer delight, a face completely open with joy for another's well-being and growth.

From that moment on, my fate is sealed, and I know that I want to spend the rest of my life with this man. Zeke is in his eighth year of recovery from alcoholism, and I am in my tenth. We've each been in previous marriages that failed, primarily because of our alcoholism. Neither of us has remarried during our recovery, instead taking the time to heal and focus solely on our own personal growth.

Zeke keeps me in stitches. He is so funny, and I'm just learning to laugh. He loves to tell funny stories and does it very well, though he often breaks into helpless laughter before the punch line, sputtering and gasping out the last few words, even sometimes falling from his chair onto the floor, completely giving himself over to his laughter.

Under the bright blue-and-red flannel shirt, Zeke's shoulders are square and broad. His hands are large with short, clipped nails. These are hands that can prepare a feast for twenty people, deftly cast a fly rod, clean and fillet a catfish, grow a vegetable garden, and artfully arrange a bouquet of peonies. More often, they are holding onto a newly admitted patient who's shaking from withdrawal symptoms or cringing from shame and remorse for landing in a treatment center for chemical dependency.

But Zeke will kneel beside them and say, "Hey! You're in the right place, or you wouldn't be here. You are exactly on time," he'll smile, looking at his watch. And then, more softly, "I don't know why some of us have all this pain, but it seems we do, to learn what we came here to learn. You're going to be O.K., my friend. If I can recover, anybody can."

One day, as I'm watching Zeke fish, he catches one, delightedly reels it in, and quickly takes it off the hook. Then he cups his huge hands around its head, presses his face and mouth over his hands for an instant, and throws the fish back into the water.

"What are you doing?" I ask, not quite believing what I have just seen.

"I'm blowing an extra breath into him to help get him started again," Zeke explains softly.

I mull this over, observing his nonchalant, easy ways, so natural, without contrivance or guile. I think, *This is who he is, the essence of him, blowing an extra breath into a living creature.*

Even a chance meeting with another person delights him. Zeke relishes everyone. No one is "too bad" or "too far gone." In fact, he seems to like working with those who are utterly lost, even to themselves. His brown eyes dance with glee, and his voice booms out, as he tenderly throws his arm across a shoulder. "Come with me. Can I get you a cup of coffee? Let me get a chair for you. Call me . . . here's my phone number."

Often, with those still wallowing in their habitual patterns of misery, he is blunt, quick, and to the point. He never offends, always honoring the spirit, the place where wholeness awaits one's acceptance of one's darkest self. Zeke has a vulnerable kind of innocence, yet he is street-wise and "spirit-wise." Other alcoholics are drawn to him, whether barnacled, blustery tough guys or shy, bespectacled intellectuals. The phone rings for him constantly and he is always available.

Zeke at the podium

My son, John, often calls him "the Ragpicker," a mystical character in one of Zeke's favorite books, *The Greatest Miracle in the World*, by Og Mandino. The Ragpicker is devoted to sifting through the trash-piles of humanity, looking for those who have been discarded and deemed hopeless, then aiding them in their struggles for renewal.

John had always been led by his intellect, skeptical of the unseen, the Divine, the spirit world or the existence of an Afterlife . . .until he met Zeke. At twenty-six, he's just finishing up law school out of state, but he visits us often. Zeke gives him frequent big warm bear hugs, and they talk and laugh for hours on end.

"Not to canonize him, Mom—besides, he's too funny, too irreverent to be a saint—but he personifies my idea of true spirit, of soul. I cannot imagine that kind of light ever going out."

Zeke just dismisses all this with, "Just passin' it on, passin' on what was given to me." The truth is, he simply adores those whom he calls the "down 'n outers." And he is clearly energized, even electrified, by these encounters. It seems that the more energy he sends out, the more he gets back. He likes the energy of sharing what he has learned about staying sober and living life gratefully and joyously. It makes him feel awake, excited and fully alive.

I've never before seen or known anyone like Zeke up close, certainly no one in my family. They all seemed to be constantly pursued by some form of "busy demon." Zeke, on the other hand, refuses to be hurried or caught up in mindless scurrying about. He's an amazing creature. He actually dares to do nothing, to fish on a creek bank and watch the water glistening in the sun for hours on end or to sprawl in a chair and lazily talk and chuckle with friends until the moon slips behind a cloud.

Often, I'll ask him what I already know about his day, just to hear it again and to marvel at his simple philosophy. "What did you do this morning, Zeke?" I'll ask innocently.

"Oh, I just jumped into my old truck and went around visiting my friends," he'll reply with a grin. "There were a few people I wanted to check on and we got talking, and I took someone to lunch who was a little down and out, and the time just got away from me."

Early in our relationship, we had talked in hushed and solemn tones about what love and commitment meant to us.

Zeke had begun with, "Do you think that two people can get past, can survive the taking-for-granted, the boredom, the power struggles, the slamming of doors, the picking and nitpicking that accompanies day-to-day living together? And what if we argue? You know arguing terrifies me!"

I understood his fear, for we had both come from backgrounds of constant conflict. Now, we each had to learn how to work through conflict in healthy ways. Hoping to remind him that conflicts might arise and that relationships ebb and flow, I said, "Maybe not. But what do you have if you don't try? Is there a rule somewhere that says we can learn how to love only with sweetness and light *all* the time? Isn't loving someone about being there and still wanting to be there on days when we don't like each other very much?"

"Well, I'm not so sure about that one. One raised voice *one time* makes me want to run," he admitted.

I sighed. "Then let us make a commitment, one day at a time, never to raise our voices to each other. I think it takes an extraordinary amount of courage to join with another unique and separate human being. Do we have that much courage?" I asked, looking deeply into his dark brown eyes.

With a big crooked grin, he said, "I do if I remember to ask my Higher Power for it one day at a time."

We saw each other as often as possible, and within four months we were married at my parents' home in neighboring Alabama. We arranged the entire event within a week. Arriving at my childhood home, we moved the furniture out of the living room, vacuumed furiously, rushed to the local supermarket, rented two large candle trees, and bought boxes of long white candles and mounds of ivy. My mother stood in the doorway, giggling at our frantic preparations.

At 7:00 P.M. that evening, we stood before my mother's minister as our two poodles wandered around at our feet. Our six grown children stood, supportive and reverent, behind us. In the flickering candlelight, we repeated our vows . . . "until death do us part."

We postponed a wedding trip and returned home the next day, the top down on the Capri, the two poodles perched on a box in the back seat. We sang and laughed and looked at each other in endless surprise that we had found each other.

Wedding day: Zeke and Jessica (center) with Zeke's daughters Sherri, Alvatti (left) and Patty (right)

It was within the next few months that I learned Zeke had been hypertensive for several years but was no longer taking his medication. He was long overdue for a checkup and an evaluation to determine whether he should continue his medication. One day, he had a severe headache and admitted that it felt like a high-blood-pressure headache. I sent him to my physician, who immediately placed him on a daily anti-hypertensive medication. This was immediately effective, and Zeke remained his energetic, jovial and enthusiastic self. However, he had a weakness for fatty foods and sweets, and his weight began to increase. I soon learned that discussing this was a taboo subject.

"Shhh . . . not now, not now . . . let's talk about it some other time," he would whisper, taking me into his arms and planting kisses on my nose.

He intrigued me. He could flash white-hot brilliance when working with others, gently reminding them of their responsibilities to self and others, yet he became a peevish toddler on the subject of his diet.

We were well into our first year together, two excited children walking hand in hand through uncharted territory in a magic forest, stopping here and there briefly, in awe that we were actually with each other and that we had come this far so happily.

One day, Zeke suddenly burst into song, accompanying the Righteous Brothers' "Unchained Melody." I walked out onto the landing overlooking the living room of our rented townhouse. There was Zeke, looking up at me from below, singing passionately in a rich deep voice, like Pavarotti's. I stood breathless, listening for a moment, then flew down the stairs and into his arms, where together we danced the last stanzas of the song.

Sometimes we practiced "bonding," an intimacy technique. Sitting cross-legged on our bed with our hands on each other's hearts, we gazed deeply into the other's eyes—not talking or smiling, just looking and feeling. Drowning in the dark liquid brown of his eyes, I would get goosebumps. I had never let anyone in so close. Nor, he said, had he.

One day, I became inspired. This wonderful man really was my husband! All day long, I wrote furiously, barricading myself behind the closed bedroom door. The two poodles grumpily scratched and sniffed at the door. The next day, I shyly handed him the product of my labor, a poem entitled "Memories for an Anniversary." He read it, beaming at me through his tears. Light-years later, I would find it again, tucked inside a folder in his briefcase where he kept only his most treasured possessions.

When my father, who was nearing eighty, died, I had had little experience with the illness and death of someone I loved.

"Come, please come, he's very ill and probably won't make it this time," I was told, and I ran crying hysterically to Zeke, jumping into his lap as he sat reading the paper. He just rocked me, folding me tightly in his arms and crooning, instinctively knowing that at that moment, I was a little girl who was losing her father.

As a child, I had been hurt deeply by my father's stony silences, his screams and yells, his mockery and hostility. I had stumbled out of my childhood almost fatally wounded and with a deep distrust of men. After several years of therapy, I had at last resolved much of my anger, fear, and hurt. Only the previous year, I had talked to him, giving that little girl inside me a voice, finally brave enough to speak her truth. My father had squeezed his eyes closed and, looking down, asked for my

Dorian, Jessica and Daddy

forgiveness. I did not give it then, but later, during his illness, I was changing his sweat-soaked pajamas and bed linen when I whispered, "I forgive you, Daddy."

His head jerked toward me, his eyes bright and pleading.

The night after the funeral, Zeke and I lay together on the root cellar roof at my mother's house, looking up at the stars. His body was warm next to mine and we lay silently, just listening to the night sounds, the crickets, a distant dog barking. We drank in the enormous black canopy of the sky above, the glittering and winking stars, feeling the timelessness, the mystery. After a long while we began to speak, and Zeke shared an experience he had had while in a treatment center for alcoholism eight years earlier. Afterwards, he had never been the same, for he had regained his hope and his commitment to life.

"It happened when I was three weeks into treatment, with only one week to go," he began. "I still could not imagine leaving there and not wanting to drink. I still did not trust that following directions would work for me. I still did not trust that I was worthy of the joy and peace that reportedly came with recovery. So one day, I found myself in my room, packing to leave.

"Suddenly, I lay back on my bed and cried out to any kind of Higher Power in the universe to please help me and to show me the way. Instantly, I seemed to be catapulted into space, darkness swirling around me. I was flying past stars, and they really *are* burning, and beautiful beings were all around me. They had no bodies, but I knew that they were beings, and their eyes—oh, their eyes! There was so much love, but the depth of it is indescribable, and they were like people I had always admired.

"It was clear that my life on Earth was only a very small part of a much larger reality. To be sure, it was important and I was definitely here to explore my life fully, to develop spiritually. I knew all these things simultaneously. Most of all, I knew that what these beings were showing me— incredible love—is what life is about. It's about learning better how to love not just others, but self. I don't know if the vision lasted five seconds or five hours. There was no sense of time. Then I was back on my bed, my face wet with tears. With a deep sense of gratitude, I began to unpack."

· We lay on the cellar roof for hours, sharing stories. I told him stories about my childhood and about my father. Then my son and my sister wandered out to join us, to talk about memories and to look at the stars.

CHAPTER TWO

LETTING GO

SATURDAY NIGHT, DECEMBER 18, 1993

I am still hearing Zeke's voice from that day; then it fades as I tear into the parking lot of St. Thomas Hospital. At a near run, I enter the brightly lit ER lobby and introduce myself to an attendant at the desk. A nurse, who seems to have been waiting, escorts me immediately to his room. He is lying on a stretcher, dressed in his olive drab Bermuda shorts. His shirt has been cut off, and he is barefoot, loafers askew on the floor. Zeke is very restless, pushing his legs back and forth and clutching his abdomen. He seems relieved to see me, but is preoccupied with his pain, and he immediately beseeches me to help him get some relief.

Olin, our neighbor, stands beside him looking on helplessly. A nurse is moving quickly back and forth around him. There is an IV running into Zeke's lower arm. He suddenly sits upright and begins to heave, attempting to vomit. I move toward him, but he pleads, "No, Honey, I don't want you to see me this way."

I am filled with anguish that he fears my seeing him so helpless, so sick, and that even now he is trying to protect me. I race out of the room to find a doctor, who is summoned by the nurse and arrives shortly. He is young and bright, and he speaks rapidly. He and his team are trying to make a quick diagnosis by elimination, and so far everything has checked out as being normal. ECG and cardiac enzymes are normal. The chest X-ray is normal.

The doctor looks at me closely. "Any history of gall-bladder problems? Is he prone to exaggerate pain?"

"No, on both counts," I reply quickly. "And the pain troubles me. I know you're concerned about drugs masking symptoms, but can't you give him something for the pain?"

He agrees, and we are all in the room when the nurse injects the painkiller into Zeke's IV line. I am standing at Zeke's side with my hand on his shoulder, and he grasps my arm as I lean over him. Thirty seconds, forty-five, one minute. Suddenly, he begins to fall back as if fainting, his color turning ashen, perspiration beading on his face, eyes rolling. He tries to speak but cannot.

The nurse and doctor move quickly, the doctor instructing the nurse to inject Narcan, a narcotic antagonist that will kill the effect of the narcotic just administered for pain. Within a few minutes, Zeke begins to respond to questions, the doctor now asking if the pain has moved or feels different. Zeke replies that it is in his left chest and abdomen. Someone puts an oxygen mask on his face while another nurse begins to prepare an IV site in his other arm.

"Let's get another chest X-ray stat. I have a hunch here," the doctor calls out suddenly. "Also, get me another ECG and a blood count stat."

Within minutes, the X-ray staff has bustled in with a portable machine, and I back away slowly to give them room. I am beginning to have the sense that Zeke is no longer mine, never again will be as I give him up to them. I feel like an intruder and marvel that they don't send me out of the room.

The scene before me seems unreal, yet I feel calm, as if I know that if I just walk through and speak my lines, I'll wake up and Zeke will be teasing me for having such an outrageous dream.

The X-ray report is back, and the radiologist adds that he can hardly believe this is the same patient whose earlier X-ray he'd seen only an hour before. Zeke's left lung is filling with blood. The latest blood count shows a substantial drop in his hematocrit. "Thoracic aneurysm," they tell me. It had ruptured just as he had been given the narcotic for pain.

When I first hear the term "aneurysm," my nurse's brain begins to clack out the thoughts: *Aneurysm. No problem. A widening area of the aorta. Can cut it out. Sew the ends together. That's that. No problem.*

Someone is tapping me on the shoulder, and a nurse beckons me out of the room. Her eyes are kind and she asks gently, "Do you have any other family members you might need to call?"

I'm looking through the open door at Zeke as we speak. A woman is standing by him and they are exchanging warm greetings, though Zeke's are very weak. I realize that he knows her; he knows everyone, it seems. I later learn that her role was to help family members in the ER arrange for transport of the body after death.

Zeke's doctor stops me as I head for the phone in the lobby. "I've just contacted the cardiothoracic surgeon on call. He's excellent, one of the best in the Southeast, and he's already ordered a CT scan of the chest. We'll have that done in just a few minutes. Its going to be a wait now for you, so you'll be shown to a private surgical waiting room on the next floor. The doctor will meet with you there after he reads the CT scan."

Within twenty minutes after I make my calls, two of Zeke's daughters, Patty and Sherri, and Patty's husband, Roger, are approaching the double doors of the lobby. As the doors swing open wide and I walk toward them, I feel once again as if I'm in a vortex, much as I had experienced

back on my unit with Bishka and Gini. We approach each
other and our eyes lock. There seems to be a knowledge
among us of all past, present and future events. I feel
completely disoriented.

Our little group is standing together in the lobby when
a hospital chaplain approaches. A young man with a
round, boyish face, he looks at us nervously. I stare at him
blankly as he shows us to a small private waiting room. An
indignant committee inside my head rises to its feet in
unison, shouting, *WHAT IS HE DOING HERE?* No one
dares to ask.

The waiting begins, the endless waiting. Fidgeting,
crossing and uncrossing the legs, being unable to read, to
concentrate. Small talk is impossible, and none of us can
voice our awful fears and dread.

Zeke's daughters' eyes are wide and shell-shocked.
The chaplain tries to make light conversation. We make
distracted, cursory replies.

Finally, someone sends him word to show us to the
surgical waiting room on the next floor. We have just taken
our seats when Zeke's doctor enters the room. He is very
tall and radiates intelligence and authority. His voice is
deep, with a measured tone, and his precise words come
directly to the point.

"I have just looked at the CT scan," he begins. "Mr.
Ezell has the most lethal of all cardiovascular conditions, a
dissecting aneurysm." He stops and coolly appraises each

of us, watching our reactions. Then he continues, "That is where the lining inside the arterial wall of the aorta is tearing, and there is bleeding between the layers that are splitting away. The surgical goal will be to cut out this area and bring the ends together with a graft, but we don't know how far down the aorta this splitting has gone. The scan is showing massive hematoma there and we will just have to see, once we get in there. He will be on a heart-lung machine. The surgical risks of this type of surgery include stroke, loss of voice, and possible paralysis."

Stunned, speechless, we dare not look at each other. The doctor asks for any questions we might have, and then tells us we can have one last brief visit with Zeke in the preoperative area. As he turns to go, I step toward him. I want to touch his hand, to look into his eyes, to say, "Please save him." I reach for his hand and he clasps mine in return. As our eyes meet, there is no need for words.

Zeke lies on a bed in the preoperative area, breathing heavily through an oxygen mask. He has been given morphine and seems free of pain. The bed with its railings is so high, I can't get close to him. I can only grasp his fingers, for IV lines and tape cover his hand.

He looks at me tenderly and then with great effort tells me that the clothes he had picked up that day from the cleaners are in the trunk of the Capri and that my Christmas presents are hidden in the bottom drawer of his bureau. And he tells me that he loves me.

Now, it's his children's turn. They are anxiously waiting to speak with him, and they murmur together briefly. Then several nurses appear, surrounding his bed and announcing that it's time to go. The bed begins to move down the hall, and I walk along beside it, holding Zeke's gaze—those dear, dark brown eyes. Seconds zoom at the speed of light into all eternity, with thoughts like small birds caught in a rushing wind and blown out to sea.

The bed picks up speed. I quicken my pace, desperation, like flames, licking at my heels. He gives my fingers one hard last squeeze.

Suddenly, his voice strong and firm, he calls out, "Jessica, I will come back to say good-bye." We look at each other for as long as we can; then the bed moves rapidly away, turns a corner and is gone.

All at once, his son, Harley, appears, having just arrived at the hospital from a town an hour's drive away. "Has he gone to surgery?" he asks frantically. "I didn't even get to say good-bye!"

"There! Around that corner!" I point. "Hurry!"

He speeds down the hallway. Later he tells me that they stopped for him, for one final, long moment.

At 11:00 A.M., a nurse from the surgical team opens the waiting room door, an elderly priest at her side. Zeke has been in surgery for eight hours. The nurse looks at us somberly.

"I have been sent to tell you that things are not going well." She hesitates, then adds matter-of-factly, "You had best prepare yourselves."

I am gaping at her, trying to comprehend her words, when one of Zeke's daughters, Sherri, cries out, "Go back and tell those doctors that we are *not* prepared. He *has* to pull through. And tell Dad, too!"

The priest remains for a few minutes, and silence hangs heavy upon the room. The girls turn away from him, furious not with him but with what his presence implies. I walk down to the patio area with him for fresh air and find myself telling him about Zeke, about his passion and enthusiasm for anyone and everyone.

After I return to the others in the small waiting room, we all kneel together in meditation and prayer to the universe, to the Higher Power in each of us, asking that this Master Intelligence of Love cradle him, have Its way with him, and allow us to accept whatever this Divine Plan unfolds before us.

A few minutes later, we're informed that Zeke is beginning to stabilize slightly.

The surgery lasts sixteen hours. Another surgeon is called in after eight hours to help route major blood vessels around the aorta with grafts. After cutting out the aneurysm, the doctors find they are unable to attach the ends of the aorta with a graft. Instead, they tie it off and begin to route the remaining portion with grafts.

When the surgery is complete, grafts will crisscross Zeke's body, connecting all major blood vessels at the neck and upper chest, descending down the length of his body and crossing his lower abdomen. It is a courageous and aggressive attempt to reconstruct his cardiovascular system by bypassing a large portion of the descending aorta.

I am still wearing the clothes I had worn to work the previous day. Now they stick to my skin. I long for a toothbrush and mouthwash, but I can't bring myself to leave the waiting room for fear I'll miss some crucial news. Nothing really seems to matter outside of the drama unfolding in the surgical suite.

I close my eyes and concentrate on the surgeons' hands, willing them, through gritted teeth, to be swift and true to their mark. I visualize healing light suffusing Zeke's body, a shimmering, powerful white light. Finally, exhausted, I curl up on a sofa, staring mindlessly at its leather back.

At 6:00 P.M., they come running down the hall with him toward the Intensive Care Unit. I can't see him for all the nurses and doctors surrounding his bed, along with several portable machines they are pushing.

As they enter the Intensive Care area, I hear one of the surgeons call out to the waiting staff, "Y'all had better not kill this turkey, we've worked too hard on him!" A tremendous sense of relief wells up inside me, for I know all too well how medical professionals, when beginning to relax about a patient's well-being, will use humor to release their pent-up tension.

Now, we're in the Intensive Care waiting room, for we've been told that we can see Zeke briefly once they get him settled in. The surgeon appears, looking very rumpled and tired. He's smiling and seems hopeful, though he admits the surgery was "precarious." He keeps his prognosis guarded, but comfortingly points out that none of the possible complications has yet occurred.

Zeke has not had a stroke. A CT scan has shown Zeke's brain to be functioning perfectly. There has been no injury to or disturbance in the nerves that govern his legs, for he is able to move them. The surgeon has also been able to identify and preserve the laryngeal nerve, so that even Zeke's wonderful voice is intact!

We are then told what to expect during the next few days. Finally, the doctor reaches up and pulls off his surgical scrub cap, says good-bye, and ambles slowly down the hall. Later, one of the nurses tells us he had come in to do the surgery while ill himself. When he got home, he rested there for two days.

Now it's time for our first visit. We are given only fifteen minutes, with just two people in the room at a time. His four children visit quickly in order for me to have more time with Zeke. I search their faces as they come out, but they reveal nothing. Their features seem to have settled into flat, emotionless masks during the long, numbing hours of his surgery.

When I finally enter Zeke's room, I am struck by his size. Ordinarily a big man, he now looks gigantic, dwarfing his bed. A moment later, I realize that this is due to his generalized swelling. The respirator noisily inhales and exhales for him. The heart monitor runs a continuous electrocardiogram, beeping with each complete heart contraction. There are intravenous tubes, chest tubes, and urine tubes. Pumps for the intravenous fluids stand like sentinels around his bed, holding fluid bags with many smaller bags attached. The endotracheal tube, which is connected to the respirator, fills his mouth, reaching down into his windpipe.

Zeke's large hands lie still. His eyes are closed, and he is deeply sedated. Reaching out, I grasp the sheet edge and gingerly lift it, peering underneath. Long incisions closed with wire sutures are scattered over his chest, and I know, from having looked at a sketch of the surgery, that large sutured incisions also cover his back. A terrifying insight flashes through my mind: *He is mortally wounded. He cannot possibly survive such an assault on his body.*

Quickly closing the door on this realization, I begin to whisper into his ear. "Hi, Honey, I'm here. And you made it! The surgery is over and oh, Sweetie, I am so proud of your fighting spirit. Hang on, Darling. Hang on."

He continues to sleep, a deep, motionless, drug-induced sleep. The nurse signals that it's time for me to go. Now that he's safely out of surgery, I turn my attention, briefly, to getting a hot shower and a change of clothes.

DECEMBER 19, 1993

I rent a room in the hotel adjacent to the hospital. Bunny, my good friend, brings me some clothes from her home near the hospital. These clothes are the most wonderful gift I could possibly imagine, other than Zeke's eyes opening and his voice booming out and his doctor's telling me that he is out of danger and going to be fine.

Soon, groups of men come, some openly crying. They are previous clients, old friends, new ones, and men he has sponsored. They come bearing gifts, food, money, but most of all, love. It shines from their eyes, along with their anguish. How deeply they love him!

Many of my friends come to sit with me, but I am so filled with the adrenalin stimulated by fear and hope, that I struggle unsuccessfully to be present, to hear what they are saying. It's like trying to speak normally to someone running alongside you as you dodge bullets on a battlefield.

The waiting room is hot and stuffy, but each trip outside seems to find increasingly bitter cold air. Looking up at the frigid, clear night sky, teeth clattering, I pray feverishly, nonsensically, babbling "Please, God, please, please...."

Every two hours, we have fifteen minutes to see him. All of his children remain; only occasionally will one or two be away. Some try to work a day or two, but they give up. Their employers are, thankfully, compassionate. The children huddle together, sometimes with me, sometimes only with each other. And they begin to talk, slowly at first, then exploding into hours of nonstop chatter. Feelings, memories, old hurts, old angers with Zeke, with each other. They smile at each other through their tears. Alvatti lays her head in Sherri's lap and sleeps. Patty leans against Harley's back as he reads. Zeke's sister, Louise, comes from Indiana. His older son, Joe, arrives from out of state. We take turns calling the house to hear Zeke's voice on the answering machine.

DECEMBER 20, 1993

The next day, it begins again. Harley comes to me as I sit shivering outside at a patio table.

"I need to talk, Jess," he moans.

Oh, God! Zeke, help me. Don't let me fail here. Zeke had agonized over this son, had longed for a deeper level of intimacy with him. I feel too fragile for this. Harley needs a therapist or a minister, not me ... not now.

Then something, someone whispers into my heart, "You don't have to offer solutions or take away his pain. You only have to listen. Just listen."

And so we sit huddled in the dark, cold night under stars so bright it almost hurts your eyes to look at them. And Zeke's son pours out his love and his pent-up anguish over his lost years with an alcoholic father, recalling how difficult it had been forgive him, despite Zeke's continual efforts to make up for that lonely time. And we cry together and decide that it is not too late for their souls to connect.

I encourage Harley to tell Zeke how he feels, even though it seems as though he can't hear.

"Tell him everything you just told me," I urge him. And so he does.

As the days fold into nights and expand again with the light of new days, I quickly search the faces of Zeke's nurses as I come in for the first visit of the day. They're usually bustling around doing their chores, their faces unreadable. The progress reports are always benign but sketchy. The real reports come from Zeke's doctor or his cardiology nurse. She has been unfailingly honest and thorough about Zeke's progress or setbacks. She comes over from the office twice a day, and if I'm not in Zeke's room she'll look for me in the waiting room. How grateful I am for her!

DECEMBER 24, 1993

Zeke's grafts are holding and his blood is coursing through them. The bad news is that Zeke is going into kidney failure. He's had very little urine output, possibly due to the prolonged surgery and ischemia, or lack of blood flow through the kidneys. I'm told dialysis will be next, and he'll be placed on the "Big Kidney" machine the next day. This powerful dialysis can draw large amounts of fluid, but only with periodic use. A smaller machine takes away smaller amounts of fluid, but runs continuously. The doctors hope that Zeke will tolerate the Big Kidney.

At any rate, I am wildly hopeful that getting his urinary output going will be our turning point. The doctor has told us that often, normal kidney function begins later. But then again, it might not.

DECEMBER 25, 1993

On Christmas Day, Zeke is placed on the Big Kidney, and his blood pressure drops. After several unsuccessful attempts, it's clear that he cannot tolerate it and will have to be placed on the smaller, continuous dialysis machine. On my first visit on Christmas Day, a new tangle of tubing is clustered at his neck, and a new machine at his bedside whirs softly. At last, beautiful yellow urine is slipping through the tubes!

Zeke has remained deeply sedated throughout our visits. "Can't we awaken him?" I continually ask the nurses.

They are evasive. One says, "It would be too much for his system. And his system needs all of his energy to heal."

DECEMBER 26, 1993

On the day after Christmas, I'm standing near his bed when I hear the strains of "Ave Maria" from a small radio that one of his nurses has brought in. The singer sounds like Pavarotti—like Zeke singing. With a chill, I look down at him. At that moment, I know for the first time that he is dying and that nothing, nothing can save him.

Panicked, I bolt from the room, grabbing John by his arm on my way through the waiting room. Fleeing to my room, I let my son hold me as I let the sobs, the grief come pouring out.

Life now becomes a veritable rollercoaster. One twelve-hour period sees improvement, while the next twelve hours show a decline. Respiratory and metabolic acidosis persists, despite improvements at times in his blood lab values. It's now becoming clear that any stability is fleeting and usually appears immediately after a change in medication. (Afterwards, looking at his chart, I see that his doctors' orders have run an average of three full pages per day, filled with constant laboratory tests, X-rays, ultrasounds, CT scans, and medication changes.)

DECEMBER 29, 1993

I begin to feel a growing sense of urgency that something needs my full attention. My fear has shielded me from the source of my unease until day ten, as I sit in the waiting room. When I open the door in my mind to its frantic knocking, I discover that Zeke is now suspended, trapped between two worlds.

And so, on my next visit with him, I cradle his face in my hands and whisper into his ear, "My Darling, I will miss you dreadfully, but if it's time for you to go, then you must. You have given me many beautiful gifts and I am so grateful for our time together. I love you so, and I will look forward to being with you again. I release you now with all my love."

My face is wet with tears as I push the words out through a constricting throat. The cardiac monitor beeps steadily, faithfully. The respirator continues to whoosh and whir. Zeke's large hands lie still.

That night, at eleven o'clock, we are all urgently called to the waiting room, where the in-house resident physician awaits us. He grimly tells us that Zeke has just had a cardiac arrest, has been defibrillated and revived. He is now considered far more critical, more unstable than ever before. Anguished, I return to my room. Yet, though frightened and grief-stricken, I also feel a profound sense of relief for him. *Perhaps he heard me,* I tell myself. *Perhaps he needed to hear my words of release.* Deep within me, an all-knowing Presence has no doubt.

DECEMBER 30, 1993

The following morning, Zeke shows a marked decline. There are now signs of internal bleeding and a "dying liver." The metabolic acidosis has increased and his blood pressure is dropping. His heart is in atrial fibrillation.

At 8:00 A.M., the cardiac surgeon calls us together. This wonderful man, who has fought so valiantly for Zeke, now looks at us sadly and says, "I'm afraid that I gave you too much hope from the beginning. There is nothing more to work with. All his systems are failing. Now we need to discuss whether to continue life support. Will it be in his best interest when there is very clearly no chance for survival?"

I quickly look around at Zeke's children, horrified, for although I have attempted to prepare myself for this possibility, am familiar with its looming black presence constantly in the background, and have given Zeke my permission to leave if he must, I now have difficulty catching my breath. Much like riding a roller coaster and turning a sharp, hairpin curve, events are now rushing us in an opposite direction, from the physical into the spiritual, into a mode of farewell. The children are looking at me and are sadly, slowly nodding their agreement that we must discontinue life support under the circumstances. We all know, without a doubt, that Zeke's surgeon would still be fighting for him if there were any hope at all. Blinking back tears, I slowly give my consent, feeling a sense of relief that I do not have to make this decision alone.

We give permission to turn off the dialysis at 8:30 A.M. They leave the respirator and the heart monitor on and tell us we can stay at his bedside until his death.

I crouch at Zeke's right side, whispering into his ear. Sherri, Harley, Alvatti and Patty surround his bed, talking to their father in anguished, spontaneous bursts. The cardiac monitor blinks its sorrowful dropping numbers, slowly, slowly, and the machine breathes for him as his heart continues to fail.

The nurse has placed gauze pads over his eyes, and I keep lifting them so that I might look into the eyes that had gazed at me with so much love. But now, the brown seems to spill out of the iris and fill the entire eye until it looks like glass. Somehow, I begin to sense that Zeke is looking at us, but that he has left his body and is up above, near the ceiling.

Finally, the Intensive Care nurse comes over and folds me into her arms. As she moves away, I see that blood has begun to trickle from his mouth. The cardiac monitor blinks 32, 30, 29, 26 and a straight line begins to move across the screen.

At 10:55 A.M., Zeke finds the doorway into the next world and is gone.

PART 2

Jessica and Daby

But ask now the beasts
And they shall teach thee;
And the fowls of the air,
And they shall teach thee;
Or speak to the Earth,
And it shall teach thee.

Book of Job
Chapter 12, Verses 7-8

CHAPTER THREE

LOVE RETURNS

LATER, HARLEY DROVE ME HOME from the hospital. Although devastated, he was attentive and solicitous. I saw his struggle to lay his own grief aside for the moment, but he kept choking on his words. It was a bitter, gray, cold day.

Fire and ice raging inside my skull had turned to molten lead. My outer skin hung in shreds. I moved slowly so as not to disturb the enormous pulsating wound that was growing inside my chest, pushing against my bones. It had jammed my mouth and eyes into a small corner where I could see only dimly and not far. My voice was flat and hollow.

Waves of hopelessness swept over me as we drove, in hand-to-hand combat with reality. First, I had to go into the house. I had not been back since we'd been there together, having stayed near the hospital ever since Zeke's admission. Then I had to visit the funeral home to make the arrangements. Then there would be the viewing of his body and the receiving of friends and family, then the funeral itself. Then ... life without him. Impossible.

Pick up one foot, then put it down. Bring up the other foot, then put it down. Breathe in. Breathe out.

As I entered the house, I felt as if I were being swept over a three-hundred-foot waterfall. I was drowning and I couldn't breathe.

Sherri arrived shortly after Harley and me and quietly slipped through the rooms. Both watched me anxiously. In horror, I realized that I needed to iron one of his dress shirts to send to the funeral home with his suit. Harley sat silently in Zeke's chair, intently shining Zeke's dress shoes so they could be taken along with the shirt and suit. The house was very quiet except for the sound of the brush against the shoes and the creak of the old ironing board as I moved the iron across the light blue shirt.

Memories flashed in my mind of Zeke cavorting around the bedroom in his shorts and socks or lying across the bed watching me, waiting, as I hurriedly pressed a shirt for him. He had never mastered the art of ironing, and I enjoyed doing those things for him. He liked doing little chores for me as well. It was all part of our giving small gifts of ourselves to each other.

I realized that I was pressing a shirt for him for the very last time. The shirt began to steam as my tears fell onto it. It seemed like hours later when I hung the shirt with his suit. How I longed to just run into the woods and scream.

Later, Harley, Sherri, and I met the rest of the children at the funeral home. John was still en route from his law office in Mississippi. Huddled together in the director's office, we numbly answered questions to assist them in writing his obituary. I kept thinking how few in number and how inadequate the words were, those words that announced Zeke's leavetaking of this world.

It should be written in the sky by squads of airplanes. It should be announced from rooftops by armies of men with megaphones, and all traffic should stop, along with radios and TVs, which will cry softly, "He is dead" and play muffled drums. How strange, I pondered, *that the world goes on as if nothing has happened.*

As we chose his casket, a stately navy blue one trimmed in silver, I kept thinking of his gay remark one day: "See if they'll let you just roll me into a soft blanket, so I can melt quickly into the good Earth!"

Sherri stayed at my elbow constantly throughout the evening. At times, when the pain rose up and overwhelmed me and the tears came, she would hold me firmly against her tiny body, rocking me gently until it had passed. John finally arrived, and the sight of my anxious, loving son moving toward me with outstretched arms was such balm for my anguish! He joined Sherri in her vigil at my side, and we moved here and there aimlessly, sometimes talking rapidly together, sometimes just sitting quietly, holding each other's hands.

Coming back from the funeral home, I was looking out over a lagoon a few blocks from the house when I noticed a large blue heron standing motionless in the water. I didn't recall ever having seen one in the area before, but it was only a sluggish passing thought that fell away to join all the rest that kept dying as they were born.

Shortly, the guests began to arrive, and the house was soon filled with visitors. Terry and her husband, Don, came with a black dress that Terry had bought for me, funded by a "love collection" from my nursing colleagues at work.

My mother and sister, Dorian, came from Alabama. Mother was still in shock and sat in silence, dazed and biting at her lip. Dorian and I went into Zeke's bedroom and I lay my head in her lap. We sobbed together for a long while, and later, I held Mother as Dorian had held me.

It grew very late and I wondered vaguely whether I would ever sleep again. The prospects weren't good. Sherri, my little shadow, lay by my side as I stared out the window at the night sky. As I began to speak silently to my Higher Power, a tremendous wave of exhaustion washed over me and I could feel myself, incredibly, sinking into sleep.

I awakened the next morning to a cold, sun-bright day, and opened my eyes for the first time onto a new world—

one without Zeke in it. I would never see him on this Earth again, never hear his voice or look into his eyes. Moaning, I pushed myself up into a sitting position. Someone you love desperately really can die—can fly from you instantly and be gone forever.

Hearing voices outside, I thought of Zeke's daughters, Patty, Sherri, and Alvatti. They had fluttered around me constantly, tearful and wise, childlike and mothering, as stunned and incredulous as I over his death. Now, peering through the blinds, I saw Patty and Sherri sitting huddled together on the river bank, looking out over the water. My son, John, was walking toward them. I leaned back on the sofa, exhausted. Suddenly their voices grew louder and more excited. Then, there was laughter, and then my name was being called urgently.

I stumbled through the door and out onto the deck, blinking from the bright sunlight. Looking down I saw, standing beside them, a large silver and white Alaskan malamute. The dog was waving her fluffy tail furiously and prancing around them, her mouth open wide in a joyful dog-grin. Kneeling down beside her, Patty was having her face lathered with licks. Then the dog went to Sherri, whom she greeted by standing on her back legs, paws on Sherri's chest, licking her face repeatedly. With John, she mischievously leapt into the air beside him at eye level. He jumped back, startled. She seemed to be teasing him! Then he, too, was receiving her generous licks of greeting.

As I approached the deck rails, looking down at the joyous tableau, the dog turned and looked up at me. At that instant, time stood still and Heaven and Earth fell silent. Shivers ran over my skin and my heart began to pound. Thoughts raced through my mind with lightning speed. *"What . . . who . . . is . . . this? This dog looks just like Zeke's beloved malamute, Baby! It's the same breed, the same color coat, the same dark-rimmed blue eyes!*

I stood looking at the exuberant animal, overwhelmed by the sudden arrival of a dog so much like Zeke's and so obviously glad to see us. Then another thought came: *It does not matter who she is or where she came from. It only matters that she is here.*

In the distance, joy raced toward me on a thousand thundering feet and swept me forward. I bolted down the stairs toward her, and she ran to meet me.

Suddenly, I flashed back to Zeke's last words. "Jessica, I will come back to say good-bye." *He did it! He actually did it!* Laughing and crying, I burrowed my face in her silky coat. She stood on her back legs once again, paws on my chest, licking away my tears. Could it be that Zeke had sent this beautiful animal to us, letting us know that his life and his love continued on, somewhere beyond?

The night before the dog's arrival, as all of us had sat blanketed under a thick layer of grief and shock, I had shared with the children what Zeke had said to me after we'd watched the movie, *To Dance with the White Dog,* only five days prior to his sudden illness—that he had asked if I desired one last return after his death, one last good-bye.

Weeks later, Patty and Sherri shared their reactions to the malamute's arrival. They had been sitting by the water for a while, each lost in her own private thoughts.

Sherri said, "I had just asked my Higher Power to help me and had then asked Dad how I could best help you, Jessica. I was afraid for you because you were so broken in your grief. Then I heard something running toward us. When I looked up, I saw a splendid white dog running around the side of the house, heading straight toward us! I remembered what Dad had said to you after watching *To Dance with the White Dog*. I didn't know exactly what this

Baby, Zeke's beloved dog.

animal's arrival represented, but it seemed to be a direct answer to the silent plea I had just made to Dad."

Patty had frequently visited Zeke when he had owned Baby, so she was very familiar with Zeke's beloved dog. She said of the malamute's arrival, "I heard fast-running feet coming toward us. It sounded like a small horse. When I turned and saw her, I couldn't believe my eyes. She looked so much like Baby, it was astonishing. Only the black markings around the face were different. I knew what Dad had said to you after the movie about the white dog and what his last words to you had been, and here was this dog! I couldn't fathom what it meant or exactly who or what she was, but a feeling of gladness swept over me, a feeling of gratitude and relief that she was here. It's hard to explain, but I knew somehow that Dad had had a hand in this."

None of us dared to share our secret thoughts at that moment, for as the joyful animal pranced among us, each of us feared that the other might deny the miracle. So we just looked at each other with wide eyes, laughing, excited, and stunned as we moved slowly, with the dog in our center, back up the steps and onto the deck. She wore no collar and her coat was filled with burrs, as if she had come from a long distance.

Patty muttered, "Now, wait a minute! I can't deal with this. I'm a Baptist. . . ."

And Sherri, touching her nose to the dog's nose, laughed and, winking, said, "Shhh . . . she's a Baptist. Can't upset the applecart."

In reply, the dog eyed Patty sharply, then licked her solidly on her nose.

As we moved onto the deck with her, someone offered, "Maybe she's hungry!"

I went quickly inside and opened several small cans of the poodles' Mighty Dog, placing the food in front of her on the deck. The dog then did a curious thing. She stood over the dog food, dropping her head low, and the lower part of her face seemed to sink into her chest. She stood very still, not turning away, but with a slumped posture, as if to be presented with such fare were to suffer the ultimate of all indignities. I had never seen a dog do such an odd thing. We remained gathered around her, marveling at her human-like stance. She ignored us and stood perfectly still, head bowed low over the food.

Suddenly, I knew what I had to do. I went into the house and brought out roast beef leftovers, and the dog immediately began to eat. *Today roast beef, tomorrow lobster. This dog gets anything she wants,* I thought happily.

I didn't want to leave her, but it was time to go to the funeral home to view Zeke's body. I was afraid the dog might try to follow us or might not be safe while we were gone. Or, worst of all, she might simply wander off and be gone—a lost dog who simply stopped by to have lunch. Reluctantly, I dressed, and Sherri, John, and I got into the car while Dorian walked with the dog as she paced around the car.

"You can't go with us just now. We need you to stay here," I called to the anxious malamute through the window as we drove away.

She struggled with Dorian as we backed out of the driveway and turned onto the street. I took one last look and saw her reluctantly following Dorian up the deck steps, looking back over her shoulder at us.

Dorian was to tell us later that when it was her turn to leave, the dog amazed her and her family by leaping onto the hood of their car and peering down at them through the glass. One and a half years later, I realized that she had never, after that incident, jumped onto a car again.

As we entered the funeral home and began to receive visitors, Harley approached me and, looking very distressed, said, "Jess, Dad would be fit to be tied if he knew how they had styled and combed his hair. It's not at all the way he usually wore it. See what you think and if you agree. . . ." He blushed slightly and looked at me apologetically. "I know it's an awful lot to ask of you, but do you think you could?"

I nodded numbly, dreading the moment when I'd view Zeke for the first time in his death-sleep. My senses, reeling, pulled the soft cushion of shock closer in order to survive.

He lay straight and stiff and formal, his body truly a shell without his exuberant spirit animating it. Yet this was the form he had lived and breathed through, and thus it was precious to me. I sat for hours looking at him, drinking in the image. I agreed with Harley that Zeke's hairstyle needed to be changed, and there were a few rough edges on his nails. He had loved to have me manicure his nails, but I could not do them just then.

I chose "Solaris Universalis" and "Novus Magnificat: Through the Stargate" for the background music during visitations. Zeke had loved to play those pieces in our Capri with the top down, offering up their soaring strains to the sky. "It's the language of the soul," he would declare, grinning as we sped along.

Soon, people began to arrive in a long steady file. The receiving room filled with flowers and the snack room filled with food. Small groups of people sat huddled together as they shared tender and funny stories about Zeke. A group of my nursing colleagues arrived and clustered around me with caressing looks and fluttering hands, speaking softly in thick, strained voices.

When Dr. Asher, our unit's medical director, arrived, I rushed forward to greet him and his wife, Nancy, as they stood in the foyer, hesitating for a moment. Embracing me, he cried, "Oh, Jessica, I'm so sorry. I didn't know you were married to Zeke. I've known him for years. I didn't see him that often, but when I did, I always loved to hear what he had to say!"

Holding me away slightly, he looked at me anxiously. "I know this is hard for you. . . ."

"Oh, Dr. Asher! It's the dog!" I interrupted, eager to share my news with him. "He said he would come back, just five days before becoming ill. And this beautiful creature came the very next day, just yesterday!"

I saw bewilderment in his eyes as he listened, and then a look of comprehension appeared. A compassionate man, he patted my hand as if to say that anything that I needed to help me through my grief was perfectly acceptable.

But I didn't need to convince anyone. It was enough that she had come, that she was here. Yes, I was walking through a fog of pain, feeling like a stranger in a strange land, foreign even inside my own skin . . . *but the dog had come.*

Before leaving the funeral home, after everyone else had gone, I asked one of the somber, dark-suited attendants to allow me time to style Zeke's hair and buff and file his nails. He seemed hesitant, unsure whether or not I was crossing a taboo line.

Sherri, hovering nearby, reassured him, "I'll be here."

So, as they stood close by in the shadows, I combed Zeke's hair in his usual style and gently buffed his nails, murmuring, "Oh, Sweetie, this whole thing is so . . . oh, Sweetie . . . oh, Sweetie."

It was time to go back home and try to get some rest, for we had another afternoon and evening of visitation before the funeral itself on Sunday. I didn't want to leave him, tried not to imagine what they would do after we left. Would they close the coffin and roll it roughly and carelessly into a dark room, a room without heat?

But he is not here, he can't feel, I scolded myself in reply to the torturous thoughts. Finally surrendering to sheer exhaustion, I let John and Sherri lead me away to the car.

As we drove into the driveway, a silver and white streak flashed down the steps and ran to meet us. *The dog is still here!* I exulted.

Our unexpected guest. Who is she—and why has she come?

We invited her inside but she declined, apparently more comfortable outside in the cold, crisp night air. She lay serenely on an old wrought iron settee on the front deck.

After dinner, we began to wash the dishes and put them away. Harley's and Alvatti's four small children were in the bedroom. Suddenly, they all came running down the hallway, feet pounding, squealing, "We saw Granddad! We actually saw Granddad Zeke! He was standing outside the window in the driveway, blowing us a kiss!" One of the children was so excited that he began to cry.

We rushed to the window, tripping over each other. The driveway lay silver in the moonlight, but no one was standing there. Yet Zeke's presence was so strong, I would not have been at all surprised to have seen him standing there, merrily waving at us.

I knew how deeply these young grandchildren had been affected by his death. He had played with them and teased them and listened respectfully to them. They had brought their sweet child-scrawled good-bye letters and their most prized baseball trophies and other gifts and placed them in the casket. Now they were tired and their emotions were frayed. Perhaps they were imagining things. Then again, I remembered that children are usually more open to the presence of visitors from the next world.

Later, the dog appeared at the glass of the French doors, and we invited her in. This time, she entered gladly. I sat with her on the floor of our bedroom. Then, lying down beside her, I said, "Oh, thank you, thank you for coming to me!" The dog reached out and touched my cheek with her paw. Someone in the room gasped, and for a long moment the room was very quiet. During that moment, those deep blue, dark-rimmed eyes held my gaze.

"Look at her! Isn't she incredible . . . isn't this incredible?" Sherri reached out, stroking her coat.

John's eyes were huge. A rational, intellectual law student, he believed every phenomenon had a logical explanation. But now, pacing about, he said awkwardly, "I . . . I guess you know that this is not a coincidence!"

With this, the dog leapt into midair at John's eye level, startling him, and he tripped, falling back onto the bed. As the dog regarded John as he lay laughing on the bed, her mouth in a wide grin, I looked around at the now-smiling faces, so grief-stricken earlier, and recognized her mission. She was to bring light into our darkness.

I was overcome by a strong urge to be outdoors. For some reason, I needed to look up into the sky, to stand by the water, so I bundled myself in several layers of clothing and went out into the biting cold. The frigid air seemed to etch out each diamond-like star with amazing precision. Millions winked and glittered from above, and I could not drink in enough of them. I felt that Zeke was now out there, had taken his place among them and was somehow a part of it all. Looking at the stars was like looking at him, and I could not get enough of them.

Two dark figures approached me. It was John and Sherri. "Where's the dog?" I asked them, suddenly missing her.

Sherri laughed. "She's still in the house romping with the kids and running from room to room."

We stood together silently by the water, listening to it splash softly against the bank. A small wind whipped in and out of the branches of the hickory-nut tree above us.

Finally, we returned to the house and saw that the children, now weary, were grouped in front of the TV, watching a movie. As I passed Patty in the hallway, she touched my arm and gestured towards Zeke's bedroom. There was a sight to behold: the dog was stretched out full length on Zeke's bed, her head resting on a small pillow. Walking on quickly, Patty wailed, "I'm afraid if I look in there again, she'll have Daddy's pajamas on!"

After a while, sleeping bags were brought out and everyone settled into a restless, dreamless sleep. Before retiring for the night, I made one last check through the house and found the dog lying curled at Alvatti's head, one large paw resting over Alvatti's shoulder. Both of them were sleeping.

I stood for a moment, watching. So! This first night she had chosen Alvatti, Zeke's youngest daughter. He had once said affectionately that Dedo, her nickname, was the "lost child" in his alcoholic family system. "She is so very special," he had mused. Then, anxiously, "I hope she knows how much I love her."

Seeing that everyone slept comfortably and that the dog was safely and snugly in our midst, I lay down, dreading the coming day and our final farewell to Zeke.

The next morning, I chose his favorite cherry-red dress for the funeral. I had worn black throughout the long visitation period, and as I pondered what I would wear to the funeral, I seemed to pick up on his wishes for me that day. I could hear his voice and see his eyes twinkling, saying, "Now, come on, Sweetie, lighten up and wear my favorite red dress! Who cares what everyone else thinks!"

The dog was eager to follow us, but we left her inside.

There was standing room only at the funeral home, and the room was enormous. People filed by for one last look at him: police officers with whom he had worked as an alcoholism counselor, friends from the music business, and an assortment of others, including an adolescent girl sobbing on her mother's shoulder.

Then, moments before the service started, a very old man slowly shuffled down the aisle toward the casket. No one knew who he was, but his clothes were in tatters. He walked alone, a vision in layers of rags. Once at Zeke's side, he took off his ragged hat and stood for a long while. Then he was gone. I was reminded of Zeke's beloved book, *The God Memo*, and John's exclamation eons ago, "Zeke is a Ragpicker!"

As the service started, Zeke's voice rang out from a cassette tape. He had recorded a short excerpt from *The God Memo*, and his daughters had chosen that medium for

Zeke to tell everyone, "YOU are the Greatest Miracle in the World."

The chaplain of the treatment center where Zeke had worked for so many years read a passage from Corinthians: ". . . though I speak with the tongues of men and of angels and have not love. . . ."

Then Sherri read a poem that she had written for Zeke.

Pure Love holds on to strangers' hands
and hearts of men of stone.
Pure Love holds on so they may melt,
their weeping stories told.
Pure Love holds on so those around
may whisper in his ear.
Pure Love holds on when all else fails
to let his children lie
upon his breast, his heart,
his head, their bittersweet farewell.
Pure Love holds on to his dear wife
through sun and wind and sky.
Pure Love holds on to the moon, the stars,
the universal lullaby.
Pure Love holds on, then gently slips
right through our mortal hands.
Pure Love holds on
and is never gone. . .
Your husband, our father, our friend.

An old friend and mentor gave the eulogy. Then Gino, a songwriter friend and guitarist, sang and played a special song that he had written. Two of our favorite songs were played, "It's in Every One of Us" and "Unchained Melody."

Then it was time for one last look, one last touch. I had chosen to keep the casket open so we could all see his physical form as long as possible. I rose unsteadily, and John and his wife, Laura, walked with me, one on each side, clutching my hand. Leaning over, I kissed Zeke lightly on his lips and squeezed his hands. Then I was being guided out through a side door into a stretch limousine that one of his friends had anonymously provided for us. *This surely can't be happening,* I thought. *It's not happening.*

The drive to the cemetery seemed endless, and the funeral procession was very long. I sat in the limo beside John and Harley, with Sherri, Patty, and Alvatti seated opposite us. We stared at each other dazedly. John kept a comforting hand on Harley and me. I knew how deeply John had loved Zeke and what Zeke had begun to represent to him, the healing that had been taking place for him, and my heart ached for him. Zeke had become far more than a stepfather to him.

John seemed intent on pushing aside some of his own grief. Yet his love for Zeke burned high, and when I looked at my husband for the last time, I saw that John had pinned a small gold angel on his lapel—a pin John had received at a time of personal discovery and courage.

As we neared the cemetery, I noticed how oncoming traffic pulled over and stopped to honor the dead and their mourners. I remembered how many times I had done so. Now I was a part of the procession of mourners, and I realized how grateful I was to experience that act in honor of my loved one.

At the graveside, Tommy, a good friend of ours, played his guitar and sang "Amazing Grace." Harley read a poem that Zeke had kept framed on his desk.

GIFT

I asked God for strength,
that I might achieve . . .
I was made weak,
that I might learn humbly to obey.
I asked for health,
that I might do greater things . . .
I was given infirmity,
that I might do better things.
I asked for riches,
that I might be happy . . .
I was given poverty,
that I might be wise.
I asked for power,
that I might have the praise of men . . .

I was given weakness,
that I might feel the need of God.
I asked for all things,
that I might enjoy life . . .
I was given life,
that I might enjoy all things.
I got nothing that I asked for,
but everything I had hoped for.
Almost despite myself,
my unspoken prayers were answered.
I am, among all men, most richly blessed!

They began to lower the casket. Unable to watch, I stood shakily and lurched toward a group of friends who were standing nearby. As Colleen held me tightly in her arms, pressing my face against her shoulder, the others gathered around, reaching out to me.

That image remains frozen in my mind to this day. It was the same vision Zeke had seen when he'd had his spiritual experience after catapulting into time and space at the treatment center in 1983. Then, beautiful eyes and loving beings had gathered around him. Now they were gathering around me.

After returning home from the funeral, we looked at the dog, still nameless. Patty and Sherri were sitting in the living room and the dog padded by, swishing her tail, completely at home with us all.

"Come back here . . . what can I call you?" Patty said, then stopped. "I can't call this dog 'Daddy'!" she scolded herself.

So with sputtering and stuttering to avoid the word Daddy and trying to call her "Baby," the name of Zeke's beloved malamute, she called out, "Daby!"

We all looked at each other. "Daby! Perfect!" I cried.

"Let's get all Zeke's pictures of Baby," my mother suggested. Looking at each picture, then at Daby, we once again fell silent, having difficulty finding words. The dogs looked almost identical.

Then everyone wanted to watch the movie, *To Dance with the White Dog*. As it began, with everyone sitting raptly in the darkened room, I looked at Daby. She was lying on her side by the children in a deep, peaceful sleep, the soul of contentment

CHAPTER FOUR

SURVIVING

JOHN STAYED WITH ME FOR A WEEK before returning to his law firm.

As the time for his departure drew near, I began to dread his leaving. Sensitive and compassionate, he had let me babble, sob, and talk incessantly about Zeke, never using platitudes to comfort, always reminding me of one of the basic principles of grief work: "Let yourself be wherever you are, and you will be carried through, not in your timing but in the timing of the process itself." A week after he left, I received a poem he had written about Zeke.

FATHER'S STEP

Lifting up as always,
Needled wreaths and terrible gifts were of no regard.
An empire of love would be yours
and a rippled history ours.
Free of gravity's rainbow,
you stepped one back and two forward.
Hard lessons for all, and
a hard-fought silence.
I can do without those stimuli now.
Today the river flows
and memories crash into furniture.
Too many strained voices asking why
to hear the whisper piercing That Day,
asking us to forgive ourselves.

The words "forgive ourselves" leapt out at me and relief washed over me. How had he known that in the darkest corner of the night, memories would arise of Zeke's visit to a general practitioner months earlier, not feeling well? Only a few basic tests had been done and a change made in his blood-pressure medication. At one point, I had thought, *Maybe he needs to go to a cardiologist, have an angiogram. . . .* But I became sluggish and never followed through with it.

I knew that guilt was a natural reaction to a loved one's death, but knowing that didn't seem to help. I was grumpy or I banged on the bathroom door that morning or I didn't kiss him good-bye or I didn't tell him that I loved him or I was indifferent, and now he is dead and I can never in this lifetime make it right.

Then there was "survivor's guilt": Why am I alive, and not him?"

I turned to journaling, a healing technique I had used for years. My days and nights took permanent form on those pages—as did my struggle to survive Zeke's unendurable loss.

JOURNAL ENTRY: JANUARY 16, 1994

The temperature is hovering at zero and the river in our back yard is frozen solid. I can't remember when I have been so cold. There is bitterness in the air everywhere. My mind feels frozen, like the ice on the water. Last night I dreamed a strange dream, feeling as if I were choking, as if I, too, were dying. In the dream, large numbers of people were choosing a gift for him, for his death. My gift was a white and frozen thing, tinged with panic. My heart?

JOURNAL ENTRY: JANUARY 17, 1994

I cannot believe that he is dead. He is not here. His clothes hang in the closet. His watch, glasses, and money clip are waiting patiently on his desk. The silence is deafening. I shove a towel between my teeth, bite down, and scream. But my heart still lies numb and refuses at times to let go. Somehow, it is all a big mistake, maybe another dream.

JOURNAL ENTRY: JANUARY 19, 1994

Perhaps the heart knows its limits and holds back the excruciating pain, letting go of only bits at a time. I sit in the bathtub sobbing as Daby paces back and forth, peering at me anxiously through the open door. Finally, she comes in and leans over the side of the tub, licking my face. Then she backs up and starts to prance playfully, as if to say, "Time's up, you've had your allotted time for crying today."

I wanted to do everything possible to keep her safe and healthy, so I drove her to Dr. David, the vet who had been watching over Peaches and Bandit, my two poodles. I wanted him to check her over for any preexisting problems and to vaccinate her to prevent future illness.

Dr. David expressed amazement that Daby would be abandoned by an owner. "Unless she has heartworms," he explained. "Many owners abandon their pets if they learn they have heartworms."

I knew she didn't have them, and a blood test cofirmed it. Then I showed him a picture of Baby and told him the story of Daby's arrival. He glanced quickly at the picture and, keeping a measured, businesslike tone, declared, "Well, she really is 100% healthy—both physically and emotionally."

Daby lay quietly on the table, resting her head on her paws and looking at him indulgently.

Bishka and her husband, El, called every day. They brought food and scented candles, ribbons for my hair, bubble bath and books by Emmanuel.

Bishka and Jessica

"It doesn't make us uncomfortable for you to cry, talk, or be silent. Whatever you need to do, we're here for you," offered Bishka, my dear friend, my light.

When they heard of Daby's arrival, they were anxious to see her and came to visit a few days later. As Bishka, leading the way, had stepped onto the deck, Daby moved forward to meet her and bowed!

Bishka came through the door with tear-filled eyes, saying, "She bowed to me!"

Daby followed them inside, staying close, moving to and fro between them.

"This beautiful dog has the most incredible presence, almost . . . almost an otherworldly presence. Those blue eyes are like deep pools of silent wisdom," El said.

Daby sat back on her haunches, looking steadily at them. Bishka sank down beside her, whispering to me, "She has been sent to you. She is a messenger."

JOURNAL ENTRY: JANUARY 23, 1994

I feel like Narcissus staring into the pool, but I am helpless under that stark and relentless gaze. Grief, by necessity, is an intensely narcissistic process. It is supposed to be and that is the natural order of things and by leaning into the raw pain, I will find healing. I trust that this is true.

Journal Entry: January 25, 1994

I am terribly ill with some kind of upper respiratory infection. I have no energy. It is a monumental task just to walk across the room. Bishka sent El over with Alka Seltzer Plus for colds, and it knocked me out for twelve hours. It was the first deep sleep I'd had since all this began on December 18. And I dreamed again.

Within the dream, I had three visitors from the spirit world, souls who had died from the Earth. Bearing gifts, they bustled into the living room from the kitchen area. There was an air of excitement and tremendous energy present. Zeke was the last of the three, rushing from the kitchen and placing his gifts on the dining room table with a flourish. There before me were three large containers of magnificent, fragrant white flowers.

I thought, "Isn't that just like him! Not one gift, but three!" His face was childlike in generosity and love and excitement, the way he had always looked when giving me gifts and surprises.

One of the visitors, a young man, told me they were also here to tell me what the afterlife was like. He sat down on the sofa while I stood before him in nervous anticipation.

"It is all very peaceful," he began. "There is absolutely no fear. We continue to grow and advance." He stood up. "This had to be brief, we must go." The dream faded.

I called Dedo and told her of the dream. She said, "Do you know what receiving white flowers from someone in a dream means? It means they are from your guardian angel!"

Putting the phone down after we had finished our talk, I thought about Dedo's statement that Zeke was my guardian angel. Somehow it didn't fit, didn't feel right. He was too new to the spirit world to take on such an assignment. I looked over at Daby lying asleep on her side and thought, *Now this one, on the other hand, might be . . . .* Be what? I always came full circle with the total mystery of her.

Once, I even asked her, bringing my face close to hers, "Daby, who are you and where did you come from?" She regarded me steadily with her deep blue eyes, unblinking, perhaps amused, perhaps thinking, "Now does she expect me to start talking, answering her questions?" Then, I flung my arms around her and cried, "It doesn't matter, my love. I am just so glad that you are here!"

Cold weather seemed to shift to a deeper level, sinking its teeth down into the Earth and holding on with grim resolution. One night in early February, as I wandered aimlessly through the house, I heard the unfamiliar sound of objects breaking, splashing into the water. Looking out of the window, I saw tree limbs covered with ice and other dark forms floating by in the river. The power went out and then the phone. We were in the middle of an ice storm.

I could not separate my grief from this cold dark world. Their edges blurred and joined. So I crept through the house on tiptoe with candles and opened the blinds slightly, as if to better see the fierce and raving monster, the icy prowler who had stolen heat and phone and light and love and now stood snapping trees like matchsticks.

Food in the power-dead refrigerator was spoiling. In the freezer, the frozen vegetables that Zeke had grown and painstakingly prepared were soggy. I dumped them from their plastic bags into a large basin, carried them back out into the garden, and emptied the basin onto the ground from which they had come.

Looking out later, I saw that Daby had taken up a vigil alongside them. She lay beside the vegetables throughout the night, her white coat catching the moonlight.

Memories of Zeke in the kitchen flooded over me. I saw him bustling around in his Bermuda shorts, every burner on the stove occupied with pots containing furiously boiling vegetables. He had a penchant for loudly banging his spoon against the rim of the pot each time he stirred. That was the scene I had sleepily stumbled upon one afternoon upon awakening for the night shift.

"Hi, Honey, what are you doing?" I asked my energetic husband, impressed that anyone could be so industrious so early in the day.

"Freezing greens, green beans, and corn! Have to parboil them first." Pulling out a chair for me at the table, he grinned. "Let me fix breakfast for you. What would you like?"

The kitchen was filled with the aroma of fresh vegetables cooking. Zeke's movements were quick and enthusiastic, and from time to time he'd look over at me with that big crooked grin. Then he gathered me in his arms, crushing me to him. He smelled of shaving lotion and soil and sun. "Oh, Jessica, I love living here! And I love you!"

A neighbor loaned me a kerosene heater, showed me how to fill and light it, and gave me some precautions on how to use it. On its top surface, I began heating kettles of water from the fish tank, and returning the warm water to the tank. My objective was to save Zeke's angelfish. They were dying, and I had become obsessed with saving them.

Zeke had been their sole caretaker. He had created the tank, carefully chosen and named each fish, and kept the tank clean and the pump functioning smoothly. His two angelfish were named Oliver and Oscar. Oscar turned out to be a bully, so each time Zeke was nearby and saw him harassing Oliver, he would tap him lightly with the net.

That didn't seem to faze Oscar, but one day he was getting very aggressive with Oliver when Zeke caught him in the act. Suddenly, Zeke reached down into the tank, scooped Oscar up in his fist, and lightly tapped him on the head! I watched in amazement.

"Stop that, you little bully!" Zeke scolded. He then dropped Oscar back into the water. Dazed and stupefied at the turn of events, the fish drifted slowly down through the water at an odd angle. Then, quickly regaining his equilibrium, he waved his tail and swam slowly to the side of the tank opposite Oliver. We never saw him harass Oliver again.

I tried to aerate the tank water by feverishly swishing it back and forth with the long-handled net. Frantic, I watched as the pair swam more and more slowly until finally, one by one, they floated to the surface, dead. Only our algae-eater remained. He became very still, conserving his energy. If startled by a tapping at the glass, he would shoot across the tank to the other side. He gave me tremendous hope: the hope that one of these little creatures who seemed to be a small part of Zeke was *not* dying, the hope that perhaps I, too, could learn how to "breathe under water."

One night as I got ready for sleep, I pulled the kerosene heater close to my bed, scolding myself for the possible risk. But the bitter cold stilled the warning voice, and I fell into a heavy sleep. Sometime in the night, I drifted up through the fog of unconsciousness, hearing a shrill beeping noise in the distance. I fought to reenter sleep, feeling very heavy and drowsy, but the beeping seemed to grow louder.

Slowly sitting up but still shrouded in a sleepy haze, I realized that the beeping was the sound of the smoke detector. Stumbling out of bed, I made my way unsteadily into the dark hallway and pulled a chair out of the dining room. Shakily climbing up and groping for the smoke detector, I located it and yanked out its battery. Once again I found my bed and quickly fell into a sweet, blissful sleep. Deeper and deeper I sank, almost to oblivion, when far away another strident sound repeatedly intruded. Trying to block it out, I reached down into the soft dark well of sleep, but was yanked back again and again by the urgent, insistent sound of barking. Crawling over the bed to the window and raising the sash, I called out, "Hush! Please be quiet!" The barking ceased and I fell back into the bed and into a deep sleep.

Opening my eyes the next morning, I lay still, bewildered and disoriented, a headache throbbing at my temples. The window remained open, a cold breeze flapping the drawn-up blinds. As my eyes began to focus on my surroundings, I found myself in a completely black room, a room covered with soot from the kerosene heater. My once-white poodles sat side by side at the foot of the bed, staring at me accusingly. The walls and carpet and furniture were black. Cobwebs in the wall corners, once invisible, now stood out in black outlines, like those for sale at Halloween. I sat up on my knees and looked into the dresser mirror across the room. Even my face was covered with fine black soot.

The kerosene heater! What had happened? I lightly brushed my hand over the now-cold metal. Had it malfunctioned and then gone out? I felt dizzy and slightly nauseated and knew these were effects of the fumes. And then I remembered the frantic, persistent barking . . . Daby! She rarely barked, but she had been lying just under the window, by the spoiled vegetables in the garden, when I'd gone to bed.

Massaging my temples, pondering it all, I knew that I could have been fatally overcome by the fumes. But I'd been spared. Had I subconsciously wanted to tempt the Fates through my carelessness?

I spent the next two weeks scrubbing down walls and shampooing carpets, but I considered my toils a minor inconvenience. It felt good and grounding to clean up my surroundings, and I welcomed the return of heat and light to my home. Perhaps one day I'd feel it inside me, as well.

I was aware of Daby's presence constantly, but sometimes, like the soot, the grief loomed black and thick. At those times, I was aware of little happening around me. Then Daby would move in closer.

In clearer moments, I would watch her intently, thinking about how she had come, how she had immediately taken her rightful place, how comfortable she seemed. She was clearly a free spirit, attached only to the universe and Mother Earth. Though always close by, she resisted constriction, petting, and baby talk. I would go for several hours without seeing her; finally, growing alarmed, I'd walk outside and call her name repeatedly. Nothing. Then, out of nowhere, she would come running toward me.

After Daby's arrival I prepared myself as best I could for the possibility that she might be a temporary gift, a lost dog whose owner might eventually surface. But even if this were true, I felt Zeke had a hand in her coming.

Reluctantly and with dread, I went to the local library to search through the past few months' lost-and-found ads. It seemed almost unthinkable that such an incredibly beautiful and rare dog did not belong to someone. Breathlessly, I turned the microfilm readers wheel slowly and searched methodically, even going back for one year.

Nothing was there.

Early one night, it began to rain—a steady, slow downpour. I glanced out the window and saw Daby sitting at the end of the neighbors' pier, looking down into the water. *How odd,* I thought, *and in the rain!*

Again and again, I went to the window. She was still looking into the water as the rain pelted down, soaking her coat. She sat there all night, as if in deep communion with the spirit of the water.

Daby had a daily ritual of visiting the park across the bridge, two blocks away. Her full white tail curved over her back, she would trot across the hill and head over the bridge in the direction of the park. Following at a distance, I would watch her loping gait as she ran along the banks of the water there, sometimes mischievously scattering a flock of squawking ducks, then watching their indignant wing-flapping as they skittered across the water. If people were there, she purposefully strode toward them, stopped for a moment to greet them politely, then quickly moved on. First she would run vigorously. Then she would move at a snail's pace, sniffing the ground. Sometimes she would lie on the bank, just watching the water.

Other times, she would join a group at a picnic table, lying quietly beside them. Daby usually ended her visit at the children's playground, playing in the sand with the little ones. She seemed to weave a kind of magic spell over other animals she encountered, even the aggressive and excited ones. They would initially circle her, growling, their legs rigid. Daby would stand very still, erect, elegant, and patient, while the other dog would move in closer. Then she'd suddenly take a playful stance, and the two would soon be romping and happily scuffling together on the grass. I never saw her become aggressive or violent with another dog.

One weekend day, she was gone a little longer than usual, and I biked down to the park to look for her. I approached an elderly man with overalls and longish gray hair. He had a kindly look in his eyes as he stood by the swing near his small grandchild.

"Excuse me, but have you seen a large white and gray Alaskan malamute here recently?" I asked urgently.

"You mean kinda like a husky or a wolf?" he asked, trying to be helpful.

"Yes. And very friendly. Have you seen her?" I tried to keep my voice even, but panic was beginning to rise in my throat.

"Oh, yeah, about . . . oh, an hour ago. She was right about . . . over yonder, with the children. Is she yours?"

"Yes, she's just a little late coming home and I. . . ."

"You'd better be keepin' her at home, ma'am. She's so pretty, somebody's goin' to steal 'er. Yes siree, she's the prettiest dog I've ever seen."

A chill ran over me when I heard the word "steal," but I thanked him and moved on, asking several other people about Daby. But no one else could give me any more information.

Discouraged, I returned home and saw that my answering machine message light was flashing. Eagerly, I pushed the talk button and heard an unfamiliar woman's voice inform me that she had gotten my phone number from Daby's collar tag. She and her boyfriend had Daby with them at their home in town, fifteen or so miles away. They had encountered her at the park and, afraid that she was lost, had brought her home with them.

I called them at once. Listening to their laughter and excited chatter about her, I thought, *Once again, Daby, you have woven your magic spell.*

A short time later, I stood watching in the driveway as their small van approached and stopped. The couple jumped out and opened the back door of the van, and Daby sheepishly stepped out. She looked relieved to see me and to be home again.

Suddenly remembering the ominous warning of the man in the park, I felt a chill of fear. Then I chided myself. *Daby is no ordinary dog. She's meant to be here. No one can steal her successfully and no ill can befall her. Relax.*

Zeke's children came out occasionally on weekends, just to be close to his final Earthly home and to visit and support me. Standing out on the deck one day, Sherri called, "Jessica, come here, quick!"

Joining her, I looked in the direction of her pointing finger. Across the river, directly in line with the house, stood the blue heron, motionless and alert. We stood watching the tall elegant bird with its long curved neck and graceful long legs.

Excitedly, she said, "I called the Wildlife Society right after I first saw her, after Dad died. They said that the blue heron was rare in this area. It's also odd that she hasn't migrated in such severe weather."

Suddenly, the bird lifted up and was airborne with a long, slow flapping of her outstretched wings. She soared back down the river, flying low over the water. Her wingspan was perhaps four or five feet, a breathtaking image. Had she come up the river to the house just to let us see her?

JOURNAL ENTRY: FEBRUARY 17, 1994

I do not believe this. He just never comes back. I sit in his chair sometimes at night and watch the glass-paneled door, expecting to see his tall frame suddenly appear, wearing the burgundy leather jacket, briefcase slung over the shoulder. I remember how we knelt and prayed to our Higher Power together. Now it feels strange that I ask this Higher Power to tell Zeke that I love him.

Sitting here in his chair, I think about his life, his journey here. He told me, with great detail, about his beginnings.

In a small coal-mining town in Kentucky in the early thirties, he led a bittersweet childhood. He played in the dusty roads and basked in the love of his grandmother until he was eight years old. Then, somehow, it began to change. He had a father who rejected and belittled him, a mother who was preoccupied with surviving her husband's emotional abuse, and brothers and sisters also straining to survive, with little energy left over for bonding with each other.

There were also frequent moves from state to state, disrupting Zeke's school years. The family had little money and even less hope.

Finally, Zeke decided that he must run away. His first attempt was brief and he returned home after a few weeks. He got no farther than the front yard that night, however, crouching in the shrubbery, watching the family occasionally move past lighted windows. He knelt there watching and crying, a fifteen-year-old child, afraid of facing an adult world alone. But he knew that he must. He wanted desperately to be protected and loved, but he also knew that going back inside the house would guarantee nothing.

And so, grieving childhood's end and eroded family ties, he sat in the shrubbery for hours. Finally, his fighting spirit returned, and he stole away into the night.

Zeke found odd jobs to earn money and learned how to drive big eighteen-wheelers. After a while, he met and fell in love with Estel, his first wife. He began to drink regularly, and his alcoholism progressed. His character defects, arising from self-hatred, grew daily, and he ached with deep mourning for his lost self, for his lost childhood. So he drank and fought and alienated all who loved him, including the five children born to him and Estel.

The Zeke that I had known was this man's complete opposite. How could one man change so much?

He had done it by reaching out to others. One day, unable to stop drinking on his own, he had sought help. He was given a plan of recovery that required him to go to any lengths to recover, to become honest with himself, and to begin the process of accepting all aspects of himself.

Once, Zeke said to me, "It is when we deny our darkest self and split it off in shame that it simply becomes repressed. Yet it is still acted out in our lives, despite our best intentions. When we embrace and accept the whole self, we begin a process of truly becoming whole."

Zeke threw himself into his recovery with everything he had. With each newfound willingness to change and grow, he reached even deeper for more willingness. His own growing freedom spurred a burning desire to share his hope with others in need. And so his life became focused on others; by continually giving, he found that he was continually filled.

Zeke began a daily regimen that would continue throughout his remaining lifetime. Each day, he meditated and asked his Higher Power that he might stay sober and continue to be willing to grow spiritually that day. He prayed that he might aid someone who needed a helping hand that day. Each night before sleep, he thanked his Higher Power for another day of living in a beautiful world and for another day of sobriety and sanity.

I remember one day last summer when he and I were wading in the creek deep in the woods while visiting Mother. We heard giggles and whispering above us, in the trees.

I said, "There must be wood fairies close by!"

"Yes! I heard them, too!" Zeke was always open to the most outrageous possibilities.

The "wood fairies" turned out to be teenagers rappelling on the cliffs above us. We called out to them, standing below and watching as the first young man came down. Perhaps ten to twelve feet before reaching the ground, his rope became twisted and he dangled, stuck in his position. Zeke immediately climbed up to a precipice and helped the boy move his legs onto Zeke's shoulders as he untangled the rope. I remember thinking at that time, "This is truly who he is, this scene before me here and now."

Oh, Zeke, and now you're gone, your fantastic bright light of humor, mischief, and compassion no longer here on Earth. The source has gone, but your light still remains in others whose lives you have touched.

And Daby is here. She is such a mystery, yet I have no doubt that she is here because of you and your promise to return. I suspect that she is an angel, an entity in her own right, yet somehow embodying some of your characteristics. What tremendous love that required, to send her to all of us, with her message of hope!

Zeke, I received another poem from John today. It is about you.

CHANCE

Even as your Earth-light faded,
Gulfs of emphatic blue
could not diminish
a chance worth saving,
I.

Fishing pole in hand,
you helped silence
the voice of false permanence,
A cunning exercise
for a brother-in-arms.

Flashes of apprenticeship
found me late.
Your monastery deserted,
I rummaged through bits of rag
you mended,
thinking only of your greeting
on my return.

How I loved that my son so adored this man who had been—would always be—my husband. And how we both missed him!

CHAPTER FIVE

GRIEVING

IT WAS TIME TO RETURN TO WORK. I had taken almost two weeks off and longed for more. I could not envision how I would function on a busy Chemical Dependency Unit with needy, clamoring patients. But I had used all of my vacation and bereavement days, and bills had to be paid. How ironic that the bereavement time given by most employers is a scant three days. This is the deepest of all wounds, the tearing away from the arms and body and spirit of a companion, a child, or a parent. And then you are expected to function normally a few days later.

Terry, my unit's Nursing Manager and an old friend, had pulled every trick in the book to buy me more time, but she had finally come to an impasse. She had left work the day Zeke had lain dying and had driven furiously for fifty miles to be there with me. After his death, Terry and Bishka had gathered all my things from the hotel room I had stayed in. Then Terry had bought me a black dress for the funeral because I had cried in her arms, saying that I was incapable of doing that.

All my nursing colleagues were infinitely patient, picking up my share of the workload without complaint. But it was time for me to return, even though I was not ready for work. I longed for stillness, for quiet. To work within chaos was battering, leaving me bruised and disoriented. As time moved on, however, I began to realize that in spite of the universality of the experience of loss, few people know how to "grieve well."

I also began to recognize that I was poorly prepared to take my grief over Zeke's loss to a healing stage. Perhaps it was because I had grown up, along with my friends, spoon-fed on values of clutching and grasping, holding on, acquiring rather than learning how to let go when the time had come.

As a child, I remember overhearing condolences offered to others, perhaps on the street or in a store or at church. "It was God's will" or "You'll be a better person from all this," people would say. Or "Don't make yourself sick grieving; he's in a better place" or "You need to stay busy, get your mind off it."

An old friend asked me, a few days after Zeke's death, "Do you think you will marry again?" So the expectation of quickly replacing a loss was a familiar one. I had seen it happen with others, creating an abrupt cessation of the deep mourning process so necessary for the healing to occur.

I had, before Zeke's death, been interested in grief work, had studied it and had begun to do grief work lectures for some patients on my Chemical Dependency Unit. While this "head knowledge" was all right for giving lectures, I found I was a novice when I actually had to do it for myself.

True, I had done a great deal of therapy during my early years of alcoholism recovery, as I grieved my childhood losses. I was no stranger to a chronic type of mourning and had felt its presence throughout my life, from childhood on. But I had not known that it was mourning, those moments of terrible longing, the feeling of having hurt someone, somehow.

And why did I sometimes have the feeling that I had moved so far away from myself that I could never go home again, never? And why did I have the sense that I was simply visiting inside my skin, and that the true occupant was a sad and angry child, grieving and in hiding. In my recovery, this child had been coaxed out into the open and affirmed and comforted. But I had never before lost, through death, someone whom I deeply loved, someone who was a daily companion.

I had long suspected, from my work with psychiatric and chemically dependent patients, that it would be easy to get stuck in one of the natural phases of grief, like depression or anger. The stage could then persist for a lifetime, unrecognized for what it really was. I didn't want that to happen to me.

I had been told that we all need a roadmap for grieving. We need to understand that it has a beginning, a middle, and an end, and we need to become aware of what to expect. Above all, we must be willing to recover from our grief, giving ourselves permission to move through the process, knowing each stage is a perfectly natural place to be. I knew enough about grief to know that it was hard, hard work and that a close and intimate confidante could help me process my thoughts and feelings.

Shortly after I returned to work, I contacted Joy, an old friend and therapist. We began a six-month grief work journey together that helped me deal with every feeling, every memory. As my "witness," she mirrored it all back to me, making it tangible and real. And as the winter melted into spring that year, I became aware that my superficial pattern of coping was through busyness.

JOURNAL ENTRY: APRIL 15, 1994

It has been a while since I have journaled. I have resisted writing; it seems to trivialize all of it.

I have bought a riding lawn mower and have mowed the lawn twice now. I have planted a small salad garden and searched endlessly for reliable men to do odd jobs. I bought a garden tiller which malfunctioned with its first use. When I called the dealer, I had a poor response until finally, after I had called him again, he said with irritation, "Don't you have a husband or a boyfriend to help you with this?"

I told the story to my stepdaughters that night by phone, and Sherri was there the next morning in a borrowed truck to take the tiller back to the dealer. I confronted him with his negligent behavior and demeaning remark and got a full refund and a long string of excuses. I have planted the tulip bulbs Zeke ordered, all two hundred of them, as well as four flowering shrubs. I broke my finger trying to pull down the garage door.

Once back at work, I faced the dilemma of what to do with Daby while I was gone. The first two days, having planned to just leave her outside, which was clearly her preference, I drove down the street with her in hot pursuit. Even though I could no longer see her by the time I reached the park, I was haunted by the vision of her running and running behind me until she was forever lost, in unfamiliar land. After the same scenario on the second day, I decided to leave her in the house with Peaches and Bandit.

Daby was not happy when I hugged her good-bye and closed the door that third morning. As I walked down the deck steps, I heard her hurling herself at the window blinds. I had left her a bowl of food and a bowl of water in the kitchen. Upon my return that afternoon, I opened the door to her wild, joyful prancing. After slowing down for one quick moment for a hug, she ran past me as I opened the door to her freedom. I walked into the dining room to an amazing sight.

Daby had eaten all of her food, then carried the bowl into the dining room, setting it down in an obscure corner. Inside the bowl, filled almost to the brim, was a yellow liquid. Disbelieving, I knelt down to get a closer look and a quick sniff. Urine! She had voided into the bowl, not spilling a drop!

Once again, the thought crossed my mind that somehow, this angelic being was still adjusting to her dog form. I had to smile at the thought of her struggle to squat over a bowl. Moving quickly toward the door, just to look at her, I saw her as I would so many times, sailing across the yard at top speed, joyful, vibrant and alive as she headed for her beloved park.

JOURNAL ENTRY: MAY 15, 1994

Now it is May. My mind races. I distract myself with doing and I forget to journal. It is extremely difficult to be still. I almost feel as if I don't deserve to rest. The flowers are blooming. I am surrounded by lush green things. But I feel small and brown and dry. I am seeing Joy regularly now. She doesn't chide me for the constant busy work. She is very interested in Daby and fascinated with the story of her coming.

It was well into spring, and Daby had been with me for nearly six months. I was becoming more possessive of her, more fearful that she would be stolen or that some harm would befall her. I kept her confined almost all the time. Generally, she met these new ground rules with a patience and serenity that always surprised me. Only occasionally did she rebel, and then only briefly and in a frolicsome, mischievous way.

While chained inside the garage one day, she found a stack of newspapers and tore them into tiny pieces, scattering them throughout the garage. When I left her in the playroom of the downstairs house another time, she leapt onto the pinball machine and was lying there sleeping when I returned and opened the door.

She often joined me when I ran errands, leaping lightly onto the back seat, where she sat upright in the corner to my right. She would frequently rest her face along the window casing as she looked out. Daby never attempted to leave the car when the door was opened, and she patiently slept if I took longer than usual in a store. Sometimes she would climb into the driver's seat and sit very straight and erect. As I approached the car, I would see her large, shaggy form leaning over the steering wheel, as if to prepare to drive us home, and I would laugh and tease her for not trusting my driving.

Sometimes Zeke's friends would stop by for a brief chat. Daby seemed ecstatic to see them, walking around them in circles, waving her tail, sometimes even standing on her back legs to greet them. Their response to her was confused pleasure at being the recipients of such a zealous greeting from a dog they had never seen before. Then I would tell them the story of her coming—what Zeke had said, how she had arrived the day after his funeral, how similar she looked to his dog, Baby. The visitors would look amazed, enchanted and then uneasy, as if unable to decide where to file this information, this fantastic possibility. So they left it adrift and changed the subject.

One day that first spring, Daby fell into her mischievous stance while a group of Zeke's friends visited me. They had gathered here to finish insulating the inside of the garage, a project that Zeke had just begun when he had fallen ill.

Daby had been highly excited by their arrival at lunch time. We were all on the deck eating when we saw her coming toward us, soaked to the skin. She had just taken a swim in the river and was moving slowly, as if to hold all the water possible within her coat. At the last second, I realized what she had planned, but it was too late to stop her. Standing in our midst, she vigorously shook herself, sending a water spray over everyone. Then she proceeded to attempt taking the food right out of the hands of the men, going from one to the other, prancing and grinning, then *snap!* A sandwich gulped down without remorse!

I had never known her to be so intrusive, but she was clearly enjoying herself and the men's attention. Zeke's friends thought she was wonderful, if a bit undisciplined. It was at times like those that I saw Zeke's influence, his puckish sense of humor, in her black-rimmed eyes.

JOURNAL ENTRY: JUNE 7, 1994

The days fly by, yet time sits on me heavily. Why, I might even live another thirty years! The thought is hardly comforting.

My life remains so unmanageable. I'm sleeping when I should be awake. I'm awake when I should be sleeping. I scrimp for weeks and then impulsively spend large amounts of money, usually for the yard and garden.

I can't relax. My muscles are in knots and my neck and shoulders burn constantly with pain. This morning, I spilled coffee granules all over the kitchen counter and floor. After cleaning them up, I spilled oats everywhere. They still remain where they fell.

When I try to talk to people, I babble. I say nothing that I want to say and much of what I don't want to say. I consider staying awake all night so I can read all the books that I have just ordered. I can't be still enough during the day to take time out to read.

JOURNAL ENTRY: JUNE 20, 1994

I had Daby shaved today due to the heat. She looks *wonderfully, beautifully, hilariously ridiculous. Now she is solid white, with a big fluffy head and tail and a shiny, clean-shaven body supported by long, spindly legs.*

I find it very perplexing that she has so little interest in food. It seems that she eats only enough to meet her basic body needs. She still cares little for dog food, so I give her wholegrain cereals, oats, rice, and cream of wheat. She seems to prefer cereals to anything else.

I have become increasingly uncomfortable with keeping her chained. I must let go of fear and let her run free. And trust that she will be protected.

I began to notice that Daby had moved in closer to me again, seeming to want to stay indoors with me more often. She would walk beside me, pressing into my legs. Perhaps she sensed that darkness was about to enter my life again.

Bandit had ballooned in weight over the past year. He was retaining large amounts of fluid that would not respond to diuretics, and he had great difficulty breathing and walking. Dr. David gently suggested, "I think it's time to show him mercy and end his suffering."

I watched Bandit closely for two more days, hoping desperately to find a sign that he could survive this episode. But it became evident by his tortured breathing that he was beyond hope.

After arriving at the veterinary clinic and settling Bandit on the table, I watched as Dr. David, always the gentle soul, approached us with the syringe behind his hand and asked me, "Are you ready?"

I nodded my head and watched as Bandit was set free from his suffering. I had visualized Zeke, who had loved Bandit, waiting for him at the end of the tunnel of Light, crouching down, his voice ringing out as in times past, "Come on, Bandit, good boy. You're home now."

I brought Bandit's body home from the clinic wrapped in his favorite flannel blanket. Daby met us on the steps with wise, sad eyes. That night, I held a candlelight vigil in the flower garden for him. As I sat by his grave, Daby appeared now and then to lie for a while by my side. She stayed very close to me for days afterward.

I soon began to realize the inevitability of Daby's own departure. I had always known on some level that I was not to have her with me for a very long time. She was only here for "one last good-bye" and to see that I survived the most acute grief-pain.

Now, each time I let her outside, I would quickly lean down, hug her, and whisper into her ear, "Please come back." Oddly, I never even considered the possibility of her death. To me, Daby was invincible.

Each night, before turning out the light, I would kneel facing her as she lay on her quilt alongside my bed. I would take her big paws in my hands and look deep into her eyes. Daby would regard me quietly, staying very still, listening.

"Thank you, Daby, for coming to me. Thank you! I am so grateful that you came!" Then, burying my face in her long, silky neck fur and giving her a tight hug, I would whisper, "Goodnight, my love."

She would watch me as I got back into bed, head slightly tilted down, her eyes slanted and looking slightly up, as if peering at me over invisible spectacles. How her presence comforted me on those long, long nights!

I began to focus seriously on my grief work. My first exercise with Joy was to review previous losses to see if there was any residue, any unfinished business. Since the last time I had worked on my losses, my father had died. Yet my previous work had resolved much of the pain I had felt as a result of his physical departure. I was deeply saddened by his death and missed his loving feelings for me at the end of his life. But I was grateful that before he died, I'd been able to accept and forgive him for having been the rageful father I had known as a child.

I discovered that Zeke's death had awakened in me a deep poignancy for all my life experiences, as if somehow they had all led me to this moment. And Joy's first exercise further clarified my own basic beliefs about feeling grief.

One theme that loomed above all the others was "regretting the past." I kept thinking, *If only I hadn't said/done this. . . . If only I had done that differently. . . .If only I had been more. . . .*

I found that *The Grief Recovery Handbook* by John W. James and Frank Cherry became my road map, along with Joy's guidance and the experiential work she did with me. Instead of just listening to my feelings, she would ask me to experience them and express them right then and there, in her nurturing presence, where I could feel safe to let them out.

Her words often followed me into a restless, fretful sleep. "You cannot successfully grieve the death of a saint. Zeke was a human being with strengths and weaknesses."

I spent many hours thinking about Zeke and our life together. We had had a brief time together, but it was a turning point for me, an arrival. More than anything else, it was a gift from the heavens. "Once in a while," as the old love song goes, we really do find love, not just someone wonderful to love us, but a fearless love rising up and out of us, often to our surprise and sometimes in spite of ourselves.

Zeke, like most of us, had been a study in contradictions —lion-hearted and peevish, responsible and careless, childlike and shrewd, wise and innocent. I began to see him as he really had been. At times, he had been frustratingly numb to my despair over finances. I always seemed to be behind on my accounting, with my sights firmly centered on "catching up."

He dismissed my concern with a wave of his hand. "There will always be bills to pay. Why fret so?"

So at times I felt very alone, hunched under the lamp at my desk late at night, trying to juggle numbers that flatly resisted me as the neon words flashed off and on in my mind: MAKE MORE MONEY. So I began a second job and became more and more irritable as fatigue set in.

Zeke viewed this as my free choice and not a necessity, gently reminding me that we would do whatever was necessary to make things manageable without my having to overwork. But my fears overruled his optimism, and I continued working two jobs.

It was late in September, two months before his death, when we took a moonlight drive with the convertible top down. We went to the Dam, one of his old haunts and a favorite fishing place. Zeke became excited as we parked and walked down the long stone steps toward the water, telling me stories of his trips there with his children. As we sat together on the steps in the warm night, I once again had the gnawing feeling, the gooseflesh thought, *You must remember this.* Driving back home along country roads, I stood up in the seat as he laughed, the headlights sweeping eerily over the dark, still woods.

My second grief exercise was to graph the happy memories above the line and the not-so-happy ones below the line. I had committed to total honesty.

The space above the line spilled over with words. Beneath the line, there was primarily our conflict over finances. Zeke had had weaknesses, to be sure, or "undeveloped areas." But in these we had complemented each other; in fact, the celebration of our differences had been the liveliness, the flame in our relationship.

There was one relentless truth that would not let go: I felt profoundly cheated that I had had so little time with Zeke that last year, primarily because I'd been holding two jobs, and our days off hadn't coincided.

And as I worked my way through my grief, I rediscovered what I had always known—that pain is a part of being in the world, that life is a wonderful drama except that it hurts sometimes. I recognized that somehow, the pain creates you anew, as if something old, though precious, is no longer needed and dies. And then you are reborn.

I became intensely curious about death and the afterlife. The stack of books by my bed grew taller—books about near-death experiences, the physiology of dying, the philosophy of dying. More exciting were the accounts of the spirits of the dead describing their experiences through mediums. Many nights my lamp burned late as I read, Daby lying by my side with slanted, sleepy eyes.

Zeke had given me many contemporary "love cards" during our time together, but one of them was my favorite. It showed an old-fashioned girl of perhaps ten, sitting on a garden bench looking pensive and wistful. She wore a white dress and a large straw hat. On the front of the card were the words, "We are always close in heart." And Zeke's handwriting on the inside said, ". . .and I am thinking of you now. I love you, Sweetheart. Z."

I pinned the card to the shade of my desk lamp.

Daby soon established her own special routine. Sometimes she rode with me to my grief work sessions, waiting, sleeping in the car until I was finished. She also selected a favorite place, a spot at the corner of my neighbor's vegetable garden fence. It was dead center on our land line. Zeke had had a minor dispute with our neighbor over the exact location of the line, and it remained unresolved at the time of his death.

Daby seemed determined to heal this rift. She made a special fuss over this man every time they encountered each other. And eventually, she won him over, enchanting him with her affectionate enthusiasm. One day, he called out excitedly to me across the yard, "She danced with me this morning, just like in the movie!"

That summer was splashed with light, shimmering in the heated colors of newly planted zinnias and marigolds, impatiens and petunias. Daby paced around, ears up sharply as I flew noisily around the lawn on my newly acquired riding mower.

I began planning with a building contractor the first phase of a project that Zeke and I had discussed. Our house was actually two houses separated by a garage. The lower-level house faced the street, while the upper-level house, built over the garage, faced the river. Zeke and I had lived in the upper level.

Zeke had moved into the original house years ago, before Patty and Roger had built the house upstairs, overlooking the water. Here he had slept and dreamed and played and worked, first alone and then with Baby. He had planted flowers here and cooked meals and fished on the river bank and taken long trips in his old fishing boat.

I could feel his energy, his masculinity, throughout the tiny house. But the building was falling into decline, and I was resolved to save it, to make it a haven of comfort, with jewel-toned colors and golden, glowing wood. I had no plans to rent it, was not even sure how I would use it, but I just trusted the feeling that I was being guided. All I needed do was to make sure that it moved in the direction, however slowly, toward being prepared.

It felt right for several reasons to spend most of Zeke's life insurance proceeds on renovating the house. First, the bulk of the restoration and face-lifting would be directed toward the house downstairs, creating much-needed room for our children's visits. I wanted to build a screened porch under the upstairs deck, with a deck walkway covered by a pergola extending from the screened porch to the planned deck behind the house downstairs.

Second, I wanted stairs built at my back door for quick and easy access to the garden and garage below, without my having to walk around from the front stairs. That summer, the back stairs, the pergola, and the main deck behind the downstairs house went up.

The next phase would be a major restoration inside the downstairs house, much of which I planned to do myself. Finally, there would be a facelift on the house's external structure, to be done by the contractor.

I pushed myself mercilessly. Working only one job for thirty-six hours a week, I spent all my days off sowing grass seed, spreading straw, weeding, watering, mulching, planting seeds, bedding plants, and mowing.

Zeke had been an avid gardener. Flowers and vegetables alike flourished under his touch. I, on the other hand, was easily confused in my attempts to decipher which was annual and which was perennial, which type of seed required which depth in planting, which plant liked shade, which sun. It had always been his realm anyway, and he seemed to like it that way, deciding where to plant each flower bed, tenderly urging the plants along as they grew.

It seemed as if everything Zeke grew somehow absorbed his energy and his reverence for life. Plants grew lush and strong, at a phenomenal rate of speed and in gigantic proportions, just to please him. I hoped that from his celestial vantage point, he was pleased by my efforts to perpetuate the beauty he had loved to create.

I bought a lawn spreader and used it to spread tick and flea killer throughout the yard. I couldn't bear for Daby to have that kind of torment, and I checked her over daily. She loathed being brushed and would playfully snap at me until I finally gave up. She seemed to have a magical way of grooming herself. Within minutes of being wet and muddy, she would bloom again in all her fluffy white and gray splendor.

One night, I dreamed of Zeke again. I was standing on a deck overlooking the woods when I saw him. He was sprawled out comfortably in a lawn chair on the bank of a creek, his head back as if resting. He had on swimming trunks and he was wet, as if he'd just come out of the water. The scene was wrapped in silence except for the twittering of birds. My hair stood on end, adrenaline surged, my heart began to pound. *It's him! It's really him. He is here!* I turned and raced down the steps. *Oh, Sweetie! I've missed you so!*

I knew it was all a dreadful mistake, a bizarre misunderstanding. Running, breathless, I arrived at the place . . . slowing . . . stopping. The chair stood empty in the silence. There was only the call of the birds.

It is said that dreams are the deepest level of healing, that the powerful unconscious, entering into our very souls, works out a solution by creating a drama that, while often shrouded in symbolism, illuminates our present struggle. My struggle, at that time, was to understand and accept Zeke's departure from my life.

CHAPTER SIX

REBUILDING

A S THE SUMMER BEGAN TO FADE, so did the final fragments of my burning energy. The constant activity began to take its toll and I grew very, very tired. I found myself focusing on the one-hundred-twenty-mile daily drive to and from the Chemical Dependency Unit, and I found it less and less bearable. I looked over my financial picture and made a daring decision. I would resign, take a few months off, and then find something closer to home.

My real impetus was my growing need to spend more and more time with Daby, to have unencumbered days with her when she could run free and not require confinement while I was working my long sixteen-hour shifts.

Some of my friends fell into pregnant silences when I announced these plans. "She needs to stay busy. The grief might overtake her if she stops," I overheard one person whisper to another at work. But I was undeterred this time, for I remained connected to that soft whisper within that always told me exactly what I needed, if I would only listen.

On September 16, having boldly resigned, I finished my last day in the unit. I drove home ecstatic. This was new for me, to resign one job before getting another. To dare to do nothing, to sit on the river bank and simply watch the water, Zeke-fashion, until the moon slipped behind a cloud.

As the air became crisper in the mornings and evenings and the leaves transformed their costumes from green to brilliant red and gold, I simply stopped in my tracks and looked around me. Everything seemed a little brighter, clearer. The flower garden was still radiant with color. The zinnias, marigolds, and four-o'clocks showed no signs of decline, and I bought plump yellow and white mums to add to those given to me by the nursing staff at my farewell party. I planted them in the front of the downstairs house in a place of honor. The sun's rays now seemed to slant like delicate fingers casting long shadows and patterns of light. Rising each morning with Daby and Peaches, I would take my coffee out to the back steps, where I sat for an hour or two. How I relished soaking in the smells and sounds of the morning. It was a time of long, slow languid days, outlined in orange and gold and drifting leaves.

O ne day, I found myself inside the downstairs house surveying the areas that needed work and beginning to make a mental list of what I would have to get.

I worked out a loose schedule for each day, promising myself and Daby that I would resist being frantic and feverish about it, that I would reserve ample time for play. I bought several sizes of sanders and brushes, sandpaper, and honey-colored wood stain. I bought wood cleaner and polish for the paneled walls and a brick cleaner for the huge, blackened fireplace.

The work was slow and tedious. Sand dust filled my hair and every exposed orifice. As I worked, Daby lay either on the front porch or outside a window so that she could see me. Sometimes, when I asked her to come in, she would step gingerly through each room, sniffing and looking around with interest. Most of the time, she just lay in the darkness outside the house, watchful and ever-present.

We spent hours together that autumn, romping on the lawn and visiting the park, I on my bike, she running along- side me. Sometimes at night we lay on the screened porch, I in the hammock, listening to the night sounds and the low, soft strains of classical music from a tape player, she stretched out on a large rug. I would look at her as she lay sleeping and silently plead, *Oh, please, please don't leave. Never, ever leave! I couldn't bear it, Daby. I can't imagine your not being here! You have meant so much, you are such a gift. Please, never, ever leave!* Sometimes, as if having heard this silent plea, she would raise her head and look at me steadily.

We took long drives in the country. One day I took her to the cemetery where Zeke's grave was located. Curious as to what she would do, I fastened a leash to her collar and gave her the lead. She began to move from the gravel lane with a brisk, purposeful stride, pulling me along. Walking past other graves, I was stunned to see that she was headed directly toward his plot! She did not hesitate or stop until she was there. Then she walked slowly around his in-ground marker and mine, which lay in wait next to his. Moving into the center of the grave, she proceeded to squat and urinate, marking her territory, claiming, "This is mine," as all dogs do. But chills ran through me as I got the distinct feeling that she was saying something more. "See? This is what I think of your rituals and customs of death, graves, markers, and such things. There is no death."

She then casually moved on, as if giving the whole thing no further thought. Riding back home, glancing at her large shaggy head in the rearview mirror, I felt the old, familiar gooseflesh prickling, followed by the same awareness: *You must remember this.*

Joy and I returned to Zeke's grave only a few weeks later. It was a warm, windy Sunday that was so clear and bright and colorful, it broke the heart with its generosity. I had written him a letter, giving words to all those remaining cobwebs of guilt and anger over his sudden leavetaking. For, defying reason, death feels like wanton abandonment, final and silent.

Joy opened the trunk of her car and brought out a large urn-like vase. We knelt together at the grave as I read Zeke the letter I'd written to him, pouring out my feelings, asking to make amends with him. I then placed the letter in the vase and set it aflame.

Joy looked at me and said gently, "You don't have to keep revisiting the guilt and the anger. You have his permission, and your Higher Power's permission, and your own permission to let it die with these ashes."

Back at the house with Joy still at my side, I took pen in hand and began to write a letter to myself, from Zeke. Although my hand and its muscles moved the pen, the words seemed to bloom from its tip with a life of their own:

My Dearest Jessica,

Thank you for your honesty. I hear what you are saying to me. Forgive me for my laxity in taking good care of myself physically. I didn't mean to die. I didn't want to leave you.

Forgive me for my shortcomings, for my procrastination, passivity, and carelessness in some areas of our relationship. I'm sorry that I'm not there for you any longer in my physical form, but our worlds do parallel, and I walk with you daily.

I have heard from Daby and others that you have grown in so many ways! I will meet you when it is your time and cross you over. So fear not, my love, for I and others will be there.

I love you truly, Sweetheart.

Zeke

I looked up at Joy tearfully, incredulously, as I finished. She was smiling, her eyes glistening with tears.

November remained almost as mellow as October. The tomato vines continued to flourish, producing ripe, red tomatoes. Zeke's house began to shine. The facings and door frames were now sanded smooth and stained anew. All the doors had been taken from their hinges, sanded and re-stained. Rusty floor vents had been taken up, cleaned, and spray-painted a glossy black. Windows were cleaned to a bright sparkle. The paneled walls glowed honey-yellow in each room. I measured for blinds and ordered them in a soft pearl ivory. They now lay stacked together in the playroom, ready for the workmen to hang. The men were scheduled to arrive in January and begin constructing a small front porch, placing light gray vinyl siding on the exterior of the house, and putting up white shutters at each window.

November marched solemnly toward December. It was time for Christmas carols and holiday decorations to herald the forthcoming holiday. The first anniversary of Zeke's death would follow right on the heels of Christmas.

One night, Daby and I went to Patty's to meet with all the children for our Christmas reunion. I had gathered many of Zeke's most familiar and precious things, finally able to give them up to his children, understanding their need for something of him that remained tangible, that could be felt and smelled and held. So I offered them his thick green robe, his daily meditation books, his collection of knives, his favorite sweaters, his favorite books. As Daby paced around in our midst, we cried and laughed and embraced each other. Although Harley could not open his parcel until he had more privacy at home, he held me close and whispered thickly, "I know how hard it was for you to let go of these."

Bishka and El were leaving town for a two-week Christmas vacation. Furthermore, they had decided to move to the coast of South Carolina. I was stunned. To lose these most loving, nurturing friends was unthinkable. Yet their move here from North Carolina had come just in time for us to feel a deep bonding before Zeke's death. Now, as if their mission had been completed, they were moving on.

I offered to rescue their dogs, King, a collie, and Gastagi, a large peke-a-poo, from the kennel for Christmas Day and keep them until their arrival home. I had just returned to work at my "old" Chemical Dependency Unit at Tennessee Christian Medical Center with Gini, Victoria, Dr.

Asher, and all the rest. So after working a night shift on Christmas Eve, I returned home and announced to all the dogs and Daby, as they gathered around me, that we would have our own Christmas party! Ushering them into the playroom of the downstairs house, I turned on Christmas carols and tied red and green scarves around their necks. I then fitted Peaches with a small pair of reindeer antlers that cupped securely under her chin. Handing out rawhide bones, I turned on the video camera and began to record. Daby lay preoccupied, chewing noisily at her bone, holding it steady with both paws. King and Gastagi, peeved with the camera's red blinking light, turned their backs to me and steadfastly ignored me as I repeatedly implored them to come to me.

"It's my bone."

It was on Christmas Day that Max arrived. I had taken a break from the party and was wandering through the empty house when I saw him standing at the glass-paneled door off the small bedroom. He was a medium-sized, muscular, short-haired dog with a ferocious look and hungry, wistful eyes. He had a short, square-jawed muzzle much like a boxer and was a golden red in color. Quivering with excitement, he seemed to know that there was a party in progress inside.

"Who are you, young man, and what are you doing here?" I demanded gently. He wore no collar and was clearly a "down 'n' outer." When I brought Daby outside to meet him, she greeted him as if they were old friends, and they immediately began to play. Upon their return a few days later, Bishka and El remarked on him. Our new addition was still with us, hanging back a little but keeping me closely within his sight. Watching him, Bishka said, "His arrival here is about . . . something . . . I wonder what it is?"

The two workman sent by the building contractor came in January and began their six-week work stint. Leonard was warm and helpful, freely offering his handyman advice, and seeming to take a protective stance with me. Jim was very young, bright, polite, and observant. They had not been here long when they asked me about Daby.

Watching her and growing faintly pink, as if surprised by his own words, Leonard said, "This is no ordinary dog. There is something about her . . . I'm afraid someone is going to steal her, with her running loose like she does."

So he bought an earth stake with a very long cord that attached to her collar. Whenever he could, he convinced her to let him indulge himself in this way. For the time being, anyway, he could feel that she was safe. Daby seemed to understand his fears and contented herself with remaining tethered, walking slowly around the yard with a bored expression.

Leonard always brought her a portion of his breakfast, picked up on the way to work from a fast food restaurant. I suspected that he was actually buying a second complete breakfast for her, for she stayed at his pickup truck eating for much longer than it would take to eat just a leftover scrap or two. The men worked steadily and efficiently, and I became accustomed to their friendly presence and the sounds of their sawing, hammering, and calls to each other.

Before my eyes, the house was transformed. It took on the look and feel of a light and spacious country cottage, even with the heavy paneling. Leonard built ceiling-to-floor bookshelves near the fireplace in the family room. He and Jim hung the blinds and laid down eggshell white vinyl in the kitchen and bath. Then, the creamy ivory Berber carpets were installed.

At last, their work was finished. I knew I would miss their cheerful presence and was sad to see them go. Leonard, watching Daby that last day, listened as I told him how she had come to us. Then he said, "I knew it was something like that with her. I'm not surprised."

As the little house neared completion, I became aware of a feeling of anticipation. While painting the bathroom a bright lemon yellow, I remember thinking, *I am in some kind of plan here. I definitely have the feeling of that. For whom am I preparing this house?*

In April, Zeke's children and grandchildren arrived for spring break, settling into the downstairs house. They fished from the river bank, read novels in the hammock on the screened porch, danced to the music of the thirties and forties on old records, and watched videos well into the night. Once, I discovered his small grandchildren on the screened porch, playing the music that had been played at Zeke's funeral, singing softly along with it as they looked out over the water.

It was a time and place for healing. Daby was constantly weaving in and out of their midst, excited by their presence. While they were fishing from the bank, she would pace back and forth beside them, looking longingly at their fly rods and fishing poles. Someone commented, "Daby looks like she wants to fish, too!" When the smaller children tangled their lines, she would give them the look that she always gave me as I flew by her on the lawnmower: "Oh, no! I can't watch!"

Daby's canine retinue had grown, for Maria had arrived in February. As I walked down the driveway one cold, rainy day, I saw a ragged form coming slowly toward me. The dog was staggering from weakness, her red coat dull, large patches of baldness showing. One of her back legs seemed to be lame. She was very thin from lack of food and looked so utterly ragged, dejected, and "down 'n' out," I thought, *I can't afford the expense of another dog! I will not look at her!*

So I silently walked past her, my head turned away. The dog stopped as I walked by, then, dropping her head, she turned around and stumbled slowly back toward the road. As I drove to town shortly afterwards to run errands, I couldn't stop thinking about her. But when I returned home, she was nowhere to be seen, so I decided to drive slowly around the neighborhood looking for her.

Please, please may I find her, I begged the universe, for I realized that to turn her away would be an immoral act. She had appeared so ill, so desperate. But she seemed to have disappeared into thin air.

The next night, I was entering the house downstairs from inside the dark garage when I stumbled over a form huddled at the door. At first I thought it was Max. Then I knelt down and saw that it was the ragged red stray, her anguished eyes pleading with me. The look of humiliation was so clear, I could almost hear her saying, "I have been thrown away and I do not belong to anyone at all in this world. No one loves me or cares what happens to me. Please, can I stay here?"

Moving toward me, she crawled slowly into my lap, pushing her nose into my armpit. I threw my arms around her in welcome.

Later, as I prepared a large, soft bed of old blankets for her, I said, "You are now home, and your name will be Maria." She fell onto the blankets and let out a tremendous sigh. Daby was there almost immediately, matter-of-factly sniffing the newcomer. The red dog's tail thumped weakly against the cement floor, and she licked at Daby repeatedly.

"Daby, do you mind if she stays?" I asked. In reply, she began to prance around the dog as if urging her to play. Then, seeming to remember that Maria was too ill to respond, Daby exited quickly and returned with Max.

Max instantly recognized her. Usually restrained in his show of affection, he went into a tailspin of emotion. He circled her excitedly, nuzzling her and licking her face for long moments. They looked so similar, I thought they must be siblings, abandoned together, and later separated. But when I took Maria to the clinic the next morning, Dr. David guessed her age at perhaps eighteen months. He had said that Max, on the other hand, was probably around five years old.

Maria was infested with whipworms, her abdominal muscles pulled up tightly in pain. Her malnutrition was so severe that her coat was falling out in clumps. Her elbows were totally bare from lying on hard ground.

"She probably looks like an older dog because she has deteriorated from neglect," Dr. David explained. "It's a miracle that she survived these past cold winter months, since whipworm infestation will prevent the body from retaining heat."

I returned home with her armed with a bag of medication, vitamins, a collar, and more dog food. Max anxiously met us as we drove into the garage. When I opened the car door, he jumped into the back seat to check her over. Before that, Max had been terrified of cars, and I had had to coax him for hours to get him into the back seat for his own trip to the clinic.

Daby stood back surveying it all with a pleased look. *What is going on here?* I wondered. *She seems to recognize them, seems to have known that they were coming.* Clearly, the dogs were familiar with each other.

In the following weeks, Maria gradually gained strength. She had lain on her bed in the garage for days, only limping outside for an occasional brief walk in the yard. Her coat began to fill in and shine. By April, her energy had surged, and she was running alongside Max and Daby as they

Max and Maria

played in the yard. Though she had a deep, forceful bark, she was gentle and sweet and would lie for hours in the front yard, looking at the house as if in ecstatic disbelief.

Both she and Max seemed in awe of Daby, the acknowledged leader, who decided when to play, when to roam, when to visit the neighbors, where to lie in the yard, and when to come inside. Yet I set a limit and never allowed Max and Maria inside the house, as I did Daby. When Daby was inside, the others would lie on the deck near the door, awaiting her next move.

It was around that time that I first met Carla. Mutual friends had introduced us one night at a get-together, and I was taken with her sweet innocence and energy, her enthusiasm for every experience. Our paths crossed again several times shortly thereafter, and we would laugh and wonder what it was all about, as neither of us believed in coincidence.

It was after we had almost collided in a bookstore that we sat together later in the adjoining coffee shop, sharing sweet time together. She asked me to be her "mentor," someone to bounce ideas off, someone to trust, to be there for her as a part of her support system. I felt honored, and we set a date and time to meet again to continue getting to know each other. We seemed to be "in sync"—in fact, it seemed as if we had met before in some other time and place and already knew each other.

One night Carla phoned, agitated. "I can't seem to work this out," she said. "I'm looking for a place to live on a very small budget, and every lead I follow seems to blow up in my face!"

She was living with her sister while completing an undergraduate degree in English and had been working as a secretary part-time. Twice, she'd been ready to move when events had occurred from out of nowhere, thwarting her. Or the prospective landlord would suddenly drop some kind of last-minute bombshell that she couldn't live with. "How strange this is," she would say to me. "It's as if I'm not supposed to do this."

One day, a thought occurred to me. *Why don't I offer her the house downstairs at a modest rental fee?* Carla became very excited when I told her, but her face fell as I explained how far I lived from where she worked.

One night, she drove out and looked at the house. "It's darling! A little rose-covered cottage, just what I've always wanted!" she exclaimed. But still uncertain about the long drive, she decided to consider it further for a few weeks.

By then I had my own misgivings, yet I couldn't clearly identify what they were or where they were coming from. It was a feeling of generalized anxiety, of impending doom, and I could not shake it.

One day, Carla called me, her voice brimming with anticipation and relief. "I'm going to move out there with you! I've worked out a budget that includes travel expenses back and forth to work. I'd like to at least try it and see how it works!"

I fleetingly considered telling her that I had had second thoughts, but because I couldn't come up with a reason for them, I tried to dismiss my sense of dread.

So my voice sounded too loud and forcefully bright, and my mouth was dry as we chattered and planned. Carla then casually mentioned that she had a dog, a small black mixed breed, and that her name was Samantha.

I don't remember at exactly what point Carla mentioned Samantha's "problem," but it was some time shortly after her move. My low-level anxiety kicked into full throttle, but once again I pushed it down. Apparently, Samantha had a tendency to fight, striking out without provocation or warning.

Carla and I decided to have all the dogs meet briefly in the yard the day she moved in. I noticed that she was nervous. Soon I realized why. At the first sight of Samantha, held by Carla on a long leash, Daby's head and ears went up sharply and she stopped dead still, watching her. Samantha seemed drawn to Daby and went rapidly to her, ignoring Max and Maria. Then she ran alongside Daby, enthralled, licking her enthusiastically.

"See!" I laughed at Carla as she stood wringing her hands in the bright sun. "They'll probably do fine together, given a little time."

I observed Max and Maria's reaction to Samantha with interest. Usually quick to check out a strange dog and communicate their prowess, they avoided her with a calm resolve. Conversely, Daby did allow her close proximity.

Suddenly, the placid scene turned into a nightmare as Samantha became a vicious, snarling dynamo. Carla jerked sharply on the leash and I shooed Daby away. Although Samantha had not bitten Daby, I had gotten a good look at two of her bottom teeth. They were long and tusk-like, one on each side. Shaken, Carla and I discussed the situation. We agreed that we would have to go very slowly with the dogs and be very careful.

"It's Daby I'm worried about," she confided, frowning, just before she marched Samantha back inside. I turned her words over and over in my mind, very, very slowly. *What did she mean by that?* When I asked her about it later, she didn't recall having said it and seemed genuinely puzzled herself.

As we settled into our new routine, I agreed to take Samantha outside for elimination on Carla's work days. She drove in to work in the morning, while I didn't leave until 6:00 P.M. Each time I took Samantha outside, she would look for Daby. I allowed them some contact but would jerk sharply on her leash if she began to growl or act aggressive.

Things began to worsen that June. It began with Daby's nearly being stolen. The first weekend in June, just before Carla moved in, Sherri had invited a group of young women over for a summer night get-together. Since some of her friends would be staying over, I readied the downstairs house for their use. I had seen Daby in the yard around 2:00 P.M., but had not seen her since. Then the women began to arrive, and I alternated between calling Daby and greeting the arrivals. It was growing late, and as I hurriedly dressed for the night shift, I asked Sherri to go to the park to look for her. She assured me that she would.

As I worked through the night, I kept feeling that Daby was in some kind of distress, and the next morning my fears were confirmed. Daby was still gone. That wasn't like her. She had never stayed out all night. I was becoming quite agitated, and Sherri apologetically told me she had been so distracted by her guests, she hadn't looked for Daby the previous evening.

All morning I searched for her, but she had disappeared without a trace. In spare moments at work, I wrote ads to place in several newspapers on Monday morning. I returned home knowing that she wouldn't be there, for the sense that she was confined had become very strong. I could almost see her prison in my mind's eye.

After placing the ads, I walked around outside for a while. Suddenly, the animal clinic where I had first taken her after her arrival popped into my mind. *I need to call them and alert them to her disappearance,* I thought. As I wandered through the yard, I saw something bright blue lying on the ground. *Oh, no! I hope that's not what I think it is.* But it was. Daby's collar lay abandoned in the grass.

So not only was she gone, but she was gone without any identification. When I entered the house again, the message light on the phone was flashing. I pressed the play button and Charlotte, one of the young women who worked at the animal clinic, began to speak.

"I'll bet we have someone you've been looking for! Call us right away."

Shaking, I dialed their number and Charlotte answered.

"Charlotte! Do you have Daby?" I cried, almost disbelievingly.

"Yes, we do," she laughed. "You can come on and get her. She's fine."

I asked no questions, just threw the phone down, grabbed my bag, and headed for the car. Once there, the girls explained that a woman had brought Daby in first thing that morning to be bathed. She was walking her on a leash and acting somewhat odd. When Charlotte saw Daby, she exclaimed, "I know that dog! She belongs to one of our clients!"

The woman became agitated and stated that she had found Daby walking around at the Dam with no collar on. She said she was claiming her as her own.

Charlotte told her, "But we will have to call the owner, you see." The woman stomped out and drove away, leaving Daby with them.

When the girls brought Daby out, she became very excited and was obviously relieved to see me. She had always ridden in the back seat by choice but that day, she climbed into the passenger seat by my side. On the way home, still very upset by the experience, I talked to her.

"Daby, I have resisted this for a very long time. But now I know that I must do it. I can't bear to think of your being stolen and perhaps abused and unable to escape, so I'm putting up a chainlink fence next week." Daby just looked straight ahead at the road, unblinking.

I had to sell the riding lawn mower and my computer in order to pay for it, but the six-foot high chainlink fence was installed the following week. It enclosed perhaps three-fourths of the lawn and provided a spacious area for play. But it was still a fence and it was still a prison.

"Daby, Daby, I am so sorry," I whispered, as the men loaded their equipment and drove away.

PART 3

Farewell to Daby

SAND-LINE

In love-lost's burning
did I conjure shameful longings
of gentle eyes
erasing a child free at last.

I and they
spend the days damming the ways
of a woodland scream.

I do not guess
the remains of past-future's reunion
will slip grave clothes that bind.

A child draws the sand-line
flying pale white overhead
and rolls the stone.

—John Roberts, 1994

CHAPTER SEVEN

ENTER, SEADOG

MEANWHILE, CARLA BUSIED HERSELF with moving in, adding her personal touches throughout Zeke's little house. Plants and rugs and delightful oil paintings appeared, and she showed me her dream journal, having drawn and painted her dreams in a bold flowing hand, splashed with vivid color.

She was childlike in her excitement and gratitude about the move. "Oh, this is like Paradise, your flowers and the water and everything. It's worth the drive!"

We had long chats late at night after she came home from work, sitting on the screened porch with burning citronella candles, pondering what had brought us together, what we were supposed to learn from each other. Since I'd begun wearing a "landlord hat," we decided that she should look for another mentor.

Carla told me that Samantha had been abused as a puppy and tearfully recounted how many months it had taken to win her over and how destructive the dog had been in the beginning. Samantha had improved in her ability to socialize with humans but generally retained a sour, aggressive disposition toward her canine family, with few exceptions.

Some days we took the long red canoe that we had bought together out onto the river and just drifted, the sun warm on our backs. We'd gaze up at white, wispy clouds in the pale blue summer sky while Daby, Max, and Maria watched us anxiously from the bank.

Meanwhile, I was experiencing a growing revulsion toward Samantha. There was something about her, even as small as she was, that was reptilian and frightening and repulsive. I realized that Carla loved her and had a long history with her, and I wanted to be fair. But my heart screamed out to banish her, to get her away from this home and yard and the safe haven that protected Daby, Max, Maria, and Peaches.

I had minor surgery scheduled for June 20, and John had offered to stay with me for a few days. After going into town to buy some of his favorite foods before dashing off to work, I found myself running late, so I hurried downstairs to take Samantha out before leaving, but for some reason, I didn't attach the leash to her collar as usual. Instead, I watched as she began to roam slowly over the yard, sniffing here and there. She seemed fine, so I went behind the house to begin pulling some weeds.

Straightening up and looking around, I found the air charged with a strange kind of energy. Heat shimmered in the air, yet I began to get a chill and to feel a bit dazed. Daby was on the deck next to me, eating from her bowl. It was then that I saw Samantha moving quickly through the garage door that opened onto the deck, headed for Daby. I opened my mouth to shout, "Get away!" but I seemed to be in a dream where I desperately wanted to scream but could not. My sluggish brain began to send commands to my legs, but they seemed to be moving through molasses. I . . . began . . . moving . . . two . . . three steps. . . .

And then she was flying through the air and was on Daby, a black fury. Yelling now, I broke through my malaise with all my strength, pulled her off Daby and dragged her into the garage, quickly closing the door. Daby stood before me shaking. Then she let out a long, eerie wail that chilled me again and broke my heart.

Crying now and trembling violently myself, I knelt down and checked her over. There was only one small streak of bright red blood on the surface of one paw. Puzzled as to where it had come from, I dug through her long coat and could find nothing. She seemed to be free of bites, with no bleeding sites, nothing.

I then quickly returned Samantha to her house and checked her over. Once again I found no sign of injury. Truth to tell, I wished at that moment that Daby had been aggressive and had fought her attacker, giving her a sound beating and teaching her once and for all that she could not cross those boundaries again.

That night, I told Carla of the incident, assuring her that neither dog had been hurt. "We can't allow Samantha outside without being on a leash or staked," Carla agreed.

Resting

The next morning, Daby entered my bedroom where, basically, she remained for the next several weeks. She left only long enough to meet her elimination needs. Lying by my side as usual, she did not appear ill and continued to eat her usual minimal amounts of food. She walked around in the house, sometimes doing her prancing and sometimes playfully teasing Peaches. She'd lie by my side if I watched TV in the living room and on the kitchen floor as I cooked. If she went outside, she was back at the door, peering in, shortly thereafter.

At first, I thought she might be frightened to go out because of Samantha, afraid her antagonist might once again appear out of nowhere and attack. But one day, Samantha got away from Carla and came up the deck stairs to our front door, looking in and barking furiously. Daby came running from the bedroom, ears up, and went nose-to-nose with Samantha through the screen door. Daby pushed at the screen, trying to get out, but I held it firmly and managed to close the French door. Carla appeared suddenly and apologetically whisked Samantha away.

My surgery went well, and I returned home groggy, relieved that it was over. I was met by a happy and excited Daby. John arrived that night and it was so wonderful to see him that I forgot about my post-op pain and prepared one of his favorites—a fresh cheese and tomato pizza, with a homemade buttery yellow sponge cake and golden peach topping for dessert. We became preoccupied with long talks, rented movies, and trips to bookstores at the mall. Daby remained in the house. Once John arrived, she began sleeping most of the time.

"This is not like her, John," I confided worriedly. "I've never seen her do this, although last summer she did want to stay in the house a lot because of the heat. Yes, perhaps that's it, the heat."

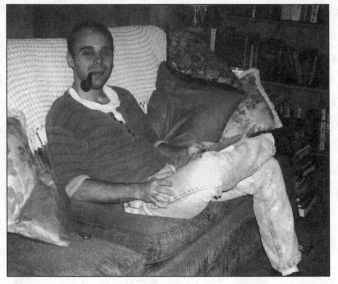
John

Regarding her with interest and smiling, John replied, "She has never been easy to figure out. Think of some of the strange things she's done. I wouldn't worry about it."

John returned home to Alabama, and I returned to work, healing from the surgery without any complications. Daby remained close by my side in the bedroom. One night, I had a highly unusual dream.

It was twilight and I was walking in the water along a shoreline. I was following a shadowy figure, a man, who was walking at a distance ahead of me. I lost my way and lost sight of him. Suddenly, I was in very deep green water. It was the ocean. Then I was high above the water, very, very high on a diving board, and I was trying to prepare myself to take the terrifying plunge. Somehow, it was imperative that I jump. Over and over, I thought, *I can do it and survive but I must remember not to struggle when I hit the water, for I will go a great distance down under the water due to the height and distance of the drop. If I struggle, I will drown. I will return to the surface more quickly if I do not struggle.*

Gripped with terror, I forced myself to look down. It was so far to the bottom, and the water was so deep and dark green, and the ocean stretched endlessly. I felt trapped, for there was no way out but through the water. Then I remembered a long-ago, ancient time when I was trapped, small and powerless, in a sea cave. The only way out was to go back under the water for a great distance to get to the opening and the outside. Tensing my muscles, I flung myself down into the abyss. Then I was falling, falling, and as I fell, a woman's voice said clearly, "Remember the Seadog, for she will always be with you. You only have to open the door and she will be there."

Tossing and moaning, I awoke lying on my side, looking directly into Daby's eyes. I was baffled by the dream. Sitting up on the side of the bed, I thought for a moment, then said to Daby, "What is a Seadog, Daby? A walrus, maybe?"

A few days later, I was lying beside Daby on the floor, talking to her and stroking her coat, when my hand moved over a lump on her side, under the skin. It was the size of a quarter, and I knew it hadn't been there before. Quickly ushering her into the car, I drove her to the animal clinic.

Dr. David, frowning, moved his hands over Daby's body as she stood patiently on the examining table. He asked for a history of recent events, and I described her unusual behavior, including her withdrawal to my bedroom during the last few weeks. Then I remembered Samantha's brief attack.

"But she didn't seem harmed at all. I checked her carefully," I insisted.

"You probably wouldn't have seen the very small puncture wounds in her skin under her heavy coat," he pointed out. "But Daby has multiple abscesses over her body, probably as a direct result of the puncture wounds. We're going to have to shave her entire body down very close, and I'll give you an antibiotic for her for the next week. It's one that bite wounds of this type almost always respond to. Then bring her back to see me in one week."

It will be all right now, the antibiotics will take care of it, I reassured myself, and drove Daby home. She ran around the yard for a while before coming in, and I felt relieved and hopeful that she wasn't that ill.

That week, however, her appetite declined, and I dutifully gave her the antibiotics as directed. The lumps, four or five of them now visible beneath her shaved skin, remained unchanged; then they began to spread horizontally.

One week later, I drove back to the clinic with Daby sitting in her usual back-seat, right-side place. Maria had come along and was sitting beside her. Four miles or so from the clinic, something told me to check the dogs in my rear-view mirror. Daby was sitting there, rigid, a startled, terrified look in her eyes. Foam was oozing out of her mouth and she was making frantic smacking motions with her mouth. Her ears were up in alarm, her eyes bulging.

"Daby?" I ventured, hardly believing this latest turn of events. I tried to keep the car on the road while I reached back to help her.

She began twitching slightly. Then the violent spasm of a convulsion swept over her and she fell onto the seat, her body stiffening and jerking. Maria, by her side, jumped into the hatchback trunk space to get out of her way.

Crying, "Oh, Daby, Daby!" I pushed down on the accelerator, praying that she'd continue to breathe without any obstructions. I screeched into the clinic's driveway, gravel flying. She was now coming out of it, dazed and weak. When I opened the door, she stepped out of the car, looking confusedly around her, and I coaxed her quickly inside where Dr. David met us.

Lifting her onto the exam table, he checked her out with a mystified expression. "The infection has not responded at all to the antibiotic. That's highly unusual, as wounds of this type almost always do. I'm not sure why she had the seizure; perhaps it's just the effect of the poisons on her system. She doesn't have a high fever, it's just a little elevated. I'll keep her here overnight, do an incision and drainage on each abscess and give her some IV fluids. Then I'll start her on another type of antibiotic."

It was time to go, so I hugged Daby good-bye and backed out the door, telling her that it would be all right, that I would return for her tomorrow. She sat very still on the table, watching me go.

Once in the car, I sat for a moment, trying to assimilate what was happening. I was extremely alarmed. Daby's course of treatment was becoming more complicated, and the seizure indicated a serious problem. The fact that Dr. David was baffled by the turn of events sent a cold wave of fear over me. A small voice told me, *Something is happening here,* but I would not allow myself to imagine the worst, that this was signaling the beginning of the end, the very thing I had dreaded from the very start.

I had always sensed that she was only a temporary gift, but it was unimaginable that she could die. It was equally unimaginable that she would simply leave, trotting off one day toward the park, that fluffy tail curved over her back as she disappeared over the crest of the hill. I sensed somehow that she would never, ever leave me in a state of prolonged agony and guessing, unsure whether or not she was in safe hands.

I spent the rest of that day and evening at home pacing mindlessly about, my anxiety growing with each passing moment. As Daby's condition continued to worsen, I felt a growing resolve. Samantha must go.

When Carla returned from work that night, I invited her to join me on the screened porch. She was anxious to hear about Daby and looked horrified when I told her of the puncture wounds and the resulting infection that was resisting treatment.

I then spoke the words that immediately brought me both relief and regret. "Though I admit that I was careless in letting Samantha run free the day of the attack, the fact still remains that she has a problem. I don't want to expose Daby or any of my dogs to even the slightest possibility of another attack. I'm afraid she'll have to go, Carla. I was hoping your sister might actually like to keep her for you. I remember your saying that she had grown very fond of Samantha during your stay with her."

Obviously distressed, Carla assured me that she would give it much thought. Perhaps she might decide that she, too, could not stay. We sat together for a while, and she talked about her years with Samantha, how difficult they had been in the beginning, how she had wearied of her many times, how it might be a relief to let her go.

Soon, she said that she was very tired and would give me her decision the next day.

I sat alone in the flickering candlelight on the porch. An owl in a nearby hickory-nut tree called out eerily. I suddenly realized that it had come here every night for the past month. Country folklore says that an owl that consistently visits near your home, calling out repeatedly, is warning you of a coming death in the family. That night, as I listened, my scalp prickled and my heart began to pound. *This cannot be. I am not ready. I cannot lose her. She has been here only a year and a half.*

I sat immobilized, looking out over the water. It was then that I saw, coming into my field of vision on my left, in the center of the river, a pair of small glowing eyes. The creature moved swiftly and steadily under the water, down the river, never wavering, on a perfectly straight course. I stood and walked closer to the screen to get a better look, remembering that long-ago time when Zeke and I had sat on the deck and had seen something similar. It had been the night we had watched *To Dance with the White Dog*. It had been the night he had asked, "Do you want me to come back . . . for one last good-bye?"

The small animal's glowing eyes were now directly in front of me, moving along on their course. I suddenly caught another movement, once again coming into view from the left. It was another pair of small, glowing eyes moving at the exact same speed as the first pair. It, too, was in the center of the river. As the second set of lights approached the center of my visual field, a third set of lights now came up on the left at a perfectly spaced distance from the first and the second. Mystified by the line of precisely placed dots of light moving under the water, I began to recognize that something magical was taking place.

I blew out the candle and rubbed at my eyes. Pressing my face against the screen, I looked at the scene before me. The river lay dark under a thin veil of moonlight. It was a partially cloudy night with only a few pale stars visible. The center of the river had become brilliantly alight with a long line of glowing eyes!

Suddenly, a light appeared near the shore and then another appeared out in the river, near its opposite bank. Soon the entire river was studded with bright lights, like stars beneath the water! I went outside and stood there, laughing through tears at the incredible spectacle. The sense of Zeke's presence was overpowering. The lights remained for a good ten minutes and I resisted the urge to run quickly to get someone, anyone, to share the awesome sight. Then slowly they began to fade, and the river once again lay dark under a pale sliver of moon.

In my wild desperation over Daby's recovery, and my wish for her to remain with me forever, I wanted to believe that the lights were telling me there was hope, to take heart. Yet, as I climbed the deck stairs to go back inside, the owl again called out its soft, haunting warning.

The next day, I watched the clock, counting the hours until it was time to pick Daby up at the clinic. I called the clinic before I left, and Renée, the pretty blond assistant, said brightly, "Oh yes! She's ready to come home!"

Shortly after my arrival there, they brought her out to me. My heart sank when I saw her. Daby's back was covered with big ugly incisions, each with a large drain and closed with wire sutures. Her once magnificent body looked gaunt and thin, for her coat had been shaved down to the skin. I knelt down and let her lick and kiss me in happy greeting. She moved slowly, stiffly, for with each step she seemed to feel the painful pull of the sutures.

Although Daby looked wretched, Dr. David seemed hopeful.

"I feel that now she will begin to improve," he predicted. "She had the antibiotics IV last night and this morning, and I also did an antibiotic wash on each lesion. The drains will keep the poisons flowing out of the body. Bring her back in one week for me to remove the drains." With this, he gave me a supply of oral antibiotics and I led Daby, still walking slowly, out to the car.

It was difficult to look at her, but Daby struggled happily into the car. I babbled to her constantly all the way home, telling her how much I had missed her and how much better she was going to feel very soon.

Once home, we slowly walked to the long deck stairs, but Daby kept stopping to look around at her incisions.

Obviously unable to climb the steps, she stood very still as I carefully cradled my arms underneath her, trying to avoid disturbing the incisions. I carried her up the stairs and into the house, then put her down and watched her walk slowly to my bedroom. Like an invalid, she lay down carefully on her quilt. I offered her her favorite creamy oatmeal and some boiled chicken, but she turned away, uninterested.

For the next few days, I carried her up and down the stairs when it was time for her to eliminate her body wastes. Even while ill, she would gingerly walk to the door to let me know what she needed. Then, standing very still, she'd wait as I carefully picked her up. Max and Maria waited anxiously outside the door, sensing that something was amiss. Once near her, they tried to sniff at Daby's drains, then hovered around her, watching her every move. She'd lick her pals quickly, then move on to take care of business. That done, she'd indicate that she wanted to come back upstairs immediately.

Once, she made a piteous attempt to trot her former wide path around the house but was forced to keep stopping, obviously in pain because of the incisions. She returned to me, and as I struggled to lift her and staggered up the long flight of steps, I talked to her, tears thick in my throat.

"Oh, my beautiful, magnificent girl! This won't last. You'll be better soon, once again running like the wind in all your splendor!"

Early that night, Carla came upstairs, smiling at me through tears. "I took Samantha to my sister's house this morning. I'm in some grief right now but I know that this is best."

She asked to see Daby. When she started through the bedroom door, Daby, lying on her quilt by the bed, began to howl. Carla quickly stepped back and began to cry. "She doesn't want me to come in! I know she's holding me responsible for what happened." With this, Daby once more pointed her nose toward the ceiling and emitted another long, plaintive howl.

Later that night, she lay quietly as once again Carla slowly entered the room, talking softly to her. She had been flatly refusing to eat, but as Carla sat by her side coaxing her, she took each bit of food offered and ate, thumping her tail on the floor. It was as if she were giving Carla a gift, allowing her to feel helpful and needed, reassuring her that she and Samantha had been forgiven. Just before Carla left, Daby lovingly licked her face.

One night, as I got ready for bed, I sat down by Daby's side and faced the dreaded truth. She was no better; indeed, she seemed worse, refusing to eat, still feverish, drinking large amounts of water. I suspected that the second antibiotic was not working either, and I knew that I would have to take her back to the clinic the next day. I would be unable to monitor her closely as the weekend approached, and I was facing twelve-hour shifts on Friday,

Saturday, and Sunday. That night, I slept on the floor, close to her side.

I called Dr. David the next day with a report on Daby's behavior, and he agreed that she should return to the clinic. Once more, I struggled down the deck steps with her, having brought the car around to receive her at the bottom. Max and Maria crowded around her, and she licked their faces in farewell. Then she looked up at the house, at the water, hesitated for a moment, then turned to allow me to lift her up into the back seat of the car.

Dr. David Gleaves

As soon as we arrived, Dr. David drew blood from her for lab tests. As he withdrew the needle, he marveled that she was always so still, never flinching from needle sticks or any intrusive treatment. But now he was clearly baffled, and I saw the beginnings of alarm in his eyes. "I fully expected her to be better by now. Instead, she's turning 180 degrees in the opposite direction. Her fever is now 104 degrees."

Dr. David was able to run some of the lab tests in his office but sent the rest out to a laboratory. He returned to us, frowning as he looked over the results of the tests he had run himself.

"This is incredible. Her blood work, so far, does not show what one would expect. She looks and acts like a very sick dog, but all these tests are normal! The BUN, the liver enzymes, everything's fine except for the elevated white blood count."

After he had sent one of the cultures from Daby's wounds out to the laboratory, he stood looking at her, nonplussed. "We will need to keep her well hydrated and give her very intensive care right now. I just don't know what else to do. I've requested tests to show any elevations for Rocky Mountain spotted fever or ehrlichia, but even if those levels are elevated, it doesn't necessarily mean she has the disease. We apparently have a good bit of detective work to do here, but we may know more when we get the lab reports back."

"What do you think it is, Dr. David?" I asked the dreaded question, afraid to hear his answer.

"I honestly don't know," he replied, shaking his head. "This is very, very puzzling."

"I have to work a shift tonight, but I'll come by to see her on my way home in the morning," I said, reluctant to leave.

He agreed, and I turned to Daby. "One more time, Daby, you have to stay."

She sat peacefully on the table as usual until I began to edge toward the door. Daby had always accepted my leaving, lying quietly on the table as I left. This time, I turned for one last look as I opened the door of the exam room, and she suddenly tried to bolt from the table, her eyes fastened on me, panic-stricken. Dr. David held onto her and I closed the door quickly and ran. The image of that moment haunted me for months afterward.

Just as we are both human and divine, in that eternal dance of balance, so was Daby both physical and divine. Since her arrival, I had watched her daily become suffused with her canine self, the wolf-like energy, the instinctive force of life with its breath of earthy, mossy fossils; with the ancient need to run and be free, to cavort in the shadows, only appearing when she chose, to lie at night on the frozen ground, straining to hear the distant wails and yelps of her canine Earth family.

Later, in the agony of my deepest grief, I described to Bishka how she had tried to follow me.

"Ah, yes . . . yes," Bishka murmured tearfully. "The Earth's sweet and fierce attachments! She did not want to let go, even for the greater union with spirit. Only the bravest of the angels come to us in physical bodies, for the blood and sinew and pounding heart are hypnotizing. The touch of skin and fur, the warmth of the sun on the back, the dreamy attachment to loved ones can become entrancing, and even the wisest of spirits will resist letting go of their physical attachments. That was her moment of resistance."

In that fleeting moment, I saw dreadful fear and perfect love in those deep blue eyes rimmed in black.

I had been Daby's mission. And the mission was nearly complete.

CHAPTER *EIGHT*

THE LIGHT GOES OUT

I THOUGHT ABOUT HER CONSTANTLY that night at work, my mind whirling. The clock hands slowed and seemed to stop altogether. An hour seemed an eternity. At last I was in my car, my shift completed, and I was driving toward her, toward the clinic. As I drove, I decided that I would seek a second opinion from another veterinarian if Daby had deteriorated even further.

The lobby was jammed with pet owners and their nervous dogs and cats. The clinic exam rooms were filled, and a feeling of chaos was in the air. I told the receptionist that I was there to see Daby and became aware that I was having difficulty keeping my voice even and clear, and I realized that I had begun to tremble.

"Dr. David is with a patient right now. If you can wait, he . . ."

"You don't seem to understand. I just want to see Daby, to see how she is."

She looked at me helplessly for a moment, then said, "I'll call Renée in the kennel and tell her." As she was calling, she began to chatter brightly about how Daby always seemed to settle in and enjoy the presence of the other dogs.

Usually grateful for any sweet prattle about her, I found myself grinding my teeth and thinking, *I do not want to hear empty chatter! I fear that she is dying.*

Renée, a tall young woman with wise, beautiful brown eyes, approached me after a few minutes, leading Daby slowly on a leash. My once magnificent comrade now stood before me, so ill that she could hardly hold up her head to look at me.

I knelt down quickly beside her. Looking up at Renée, I said, "I cannot, *will* not stand idly by watching her die. I have decided to take her to the veterinarian that I used with the poodles when I lived in Gallatin."

Renée looked at me sadly and whispered, "Wait. Let me see if I can get Dr. David."

The room began to feel stuffy, crowded with the chaotic background din of barking dogs and meowing cats. I led Daby out and knelt down again beside her.

Within a few minutes, Dr. David came rushing out, his face red and his eyes anguished, talking rapidly. "I'm sorry I couldn't get to you when you first came in but the clinic is overflowing with patients this morning. I know she's worse, but I've done everything I know how to do! And the lab reports are not back yet and...."

"But Dr. David, she's dying," I cried. "I cannot stand by and do nothing! I must make some effort to save her!"

Turning away sadly, he said, "Well then, do what you must. But I'll call you with the results of the lab tests as soon as they come in. The culture report takes longer and won't be in until Monday."

As I walked Daby slowly to the car, I glimpsed the faces of Renée, Charlotte, and several others at the office window. They seemed to be giving Daby a long, lingering look of sad farewell, for from the beginning they had been captivated by Zeke's promise to me, her arrival the day after, and her strong resemblance to Baby.

As I drove the fifty miles to Gallatin with her, I kept looking back at her, babbling constantly, crying, "Oh, my sweet girl! I am so sorry, so very sorry that you are having to experience this. Dr. McMillan may have the answers for us; he's been practicing for a long time. He may have treated something similar. Hang on, hang on."

She sat very still there in the back seat, struggling to hold up her head to look at me. Once again, it was "that look." Her head down slightly, she looked up at me with slanted eyes over invisible spectacles. Only this time, I saw indescribable sorrow in her eyes.

As I led her into Dr. McMillan's waiting room, I was again greeted with barks and growls and meows. Seeing that the waiting room was full, I signed us in, asking that we be seen right away, as Daby was so ill. Leaning against the wall with Daby pressing in against my legs, I looked around the room. The people there were looking at Daby in alarm and then back at me with sympathy. I looked quickly away, for I did not want to invite idle conversation. I just couldn't form casual words or make polite responses.

Within a few minutes, we were ushered into an exam room, and Dr. McMillan bustled into the room behind us. He always moved quickly and spoke with a passion for whatever he was involved in. I told him in detail of the events that had led to her illness and of the treatment given her so far.

Immediately, he took her temperature and grimaced at what he saw when he withdrew the thermometer. "The first thing is to get that fever down and make her as comfortable as possible while I decide what to do next!"

He gave her an injection of something to lower her temperature and then led us over to a large drain board covering a tremendous sink. Lifting Daby up onto the drain board, he turned and pulled over a tall stool for me to perch on beside her.

"Now, let me show you what to do. Turn the warm water on like this, letting it flow through the spray nozzle on the wand, and keep running the warm water over the incisions on her back. This will ease the pain and pulling of the wounds. I've had wonderful results with hydrotherapy."

For what seemed hours, I sat very close to her, running the warm water over her wounds as she lay on the drain board. Daby kept her head very still in my lap, her eyes open, surveying the room as Dr. McMillan rushed here and there, taking care of other patients. I stroked the silky fur around her face and talked to her, and she lay there quietly with complete acceptance.

Dr. McMillan gave her several more injections and started a bag of intravenous fluids. As he sank the needle and syringe into her leg to draw blood for more lab tests, he

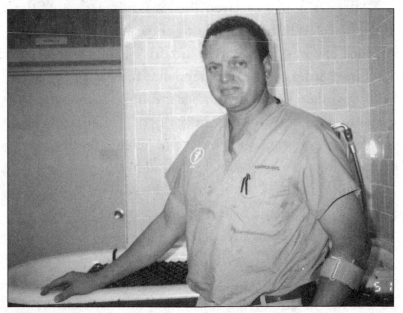

Dr. Jerry McMillan

looked up at me incredulously. "Has she always been this laid back?!"

I told him of the lab tests that were still out and of those Dr. David had done in his office. Dr. McMillan then ran the same tests himself and returned to the room, saying, "Same thing. They were all normal. How very strange."

He decided on an antibiotic that he had used once in a case that had stubbornly resisted all other drugs. The dog, near death, had recovered.

Hope began to tap a steady, cadenced drumbeat in my heart.

After Daby had received the IV fluids, Dr. McMillan suggested I walk her outside to allow her to relieve her bladder. She was now clearly more frisky, and I was elated. Holding her leash with one hand and the bag of IV fluids with the other, I moved with her through the lobby to the outside of the building. She voided immediately and sniffed at the grass and the earth. Then, standing very still, she looked ever so slowly around her.

Taking her back inside to Dr. McMillan, I told him excitedly, "She seems to feel so much better! Her pace is quicker and she seems stronger!"

He, too, looked hopeful. "I don't know for sure that this will work, but we'll give it all we've got. I'm going to put her in one of the cages now, and you can be on your way."

I hesitated. But she seemed so much better, I decided to leave her for a while. "Please call me later tonight with news of her, or sooner if her condition worsens. In that case, I must be with her," I insisted.

He readily agreed, and I gave him my home phone number and my work number. As we entered the hospital kennel room, he moved her toward a small cage, the only one available. Her seemingly dramatic improvement had heartened me so, I didn't protest. Daby leaned down slightly and walked into the cage without hesitation. Turning around with difficulty, she lay facing us as the door was closed behind her.

"She loves a fan on her, turned low. Could you please . . . do you have one?" I begged.

"Oh, yes, indeed. I'll put one near her immediately," Dr. McMillan promised.

I knelt before her, touching her long nose with my fingers through the wire. Tears were welling up again, but this time they were filled with blessed, beautiful hope.

"Daby, oh, Daby, how I hate to leave you! But I will be back for you soon. You are getting better now and Dr. McMillan has been instructed to call me if you start to feel bad again."

She stared back at me deeply with those incredible eyes, so startlingly blue. At that moment her eyes were very, very peaceful.

"Good-bye, my love," I whispered as I went through the door.

Outside the room, I beseeched Dr. McMillan again to please, please take good care of her, that I didn't have time right then, nor did he, for me to tell him the story of how she had come to me, but I would tell him later. And I asked him to please call me if there was any change at all.

Driving home, I vacillated between wild elation that she seemed to be improving and intense fear and dread. Dr. McMillan called at 6:00 P.M. as I was dressing for work. His voice was bright and he sounded eager and happy to report that Daby had eaten an entire can of dog food for him. I was amazed, for she hadn't done that even when in excellent health. And yes, he had the fan on her.

I was so relieved that I hardly knew where I was, whether driving to work or going into the hospital or beginning to organize the chores awaiting me.

And then I was called to the phone. It was Dr. David, his voice very warm and calm. He had the lab results, and slowly read them out to me as I wrote them down. They were also normal, except for the Rocky Mountain spotted fever and ehrlichia titers. But although somewhat elevated, they weren't high enough to indicate that she had either disease.

"All of this is very puzzling," he pondered. "The pieces just don't fit."

"I'm grateful for your calling me with these results and for all the work you've done for her. I just felt that I had to get another opinion," I concluded apologetically.

I told him that Daby seemed much better, and he sounded very relieved to hear that. Then he asked if I minded his calling Dr. McMillan to discuss the case with him.

I was very moved. "Please do!" I invited, grateful for his concern.

When I returned home the next morning, my phone message light was flashing. It was Dr. McMillan, asking that I beep him for a progress report on Daby. I did so right away and his voice was calm, but I detected an undercurrent of concern.

"There's been a change in her breathing. I sat in front of her cage for twenty minutes this morning watching her breathe. There is a tiny gasp every now and then."

"Change in breathing?! Doesn't that mean that I need to come right away?"

"No, no, that's not necessary. You get some rest, you've been working all night. I'll keep you posted. It's just a small, slight gasp occasionally."

I gave him the lab results from Dr. David.

"I feel encouraged by these reports," Dr. McMillian admitted. "I'll call you if there is any change. Now get some rest. I'll call you again tonight at 6:00 P.M.

Reluctantly, I hung up the phone, then sat thinking for a minute before I picked up the receiver again. Calling Staffing at the hospital, I informed them that I was ill and wouldn't be in that night. I knew that was the surest way to place my job in safekeeping, for if the call came to me at work that she was dying, I would leave immediately. If they could not accept my reason for leaving, I would have to resign on the spot and leave anyway.

Dr. McMillan called at exactly 6:00 P.M. to tell me that there had been no change. She was drinking water and had eaten a bit more. The tiny, occasional gasps were still there. Again, I queried him about my going there, telling him I'd taken the night off in case I was needed, that I would just sit quietly with her and stay out of everyone's way.

"Oh, no," he said quickly. "That isn't necessary. She'll be O.K. Her lab work is essentially normal and this isn't real dyspnea breathing distress. Just be here early in the morning."

Despite his words of reassurance, I couldn't sleep. I kept seeing Daby's face through the wire of the small cage. At 2:00 A.M., I drifted off but leapt out of bed at 6:00 A.M. Dressing quickly, I packed a large satchel with a change of clothes, a few books, a thermos of coffee, and a sandwich. I planned to stay with Daby for as long as Dr. McMillan would let me, or at least I would stay nearby in a hotel.

As I drove toward Gallatin that morning, I was electrified with apprehension and dread and hope. Suddenly, about five miles from her, a gigantic bird, much like a hawk or an eagle, flew down directly in front of me, as close as the car hood's nose, a rustle of majestic, winged speed. It turned and looked directly at me, a fleeting, stern, compassionate stare. The look was unmistakable. *Brace yourself.*

I gripped the wheel and strained to follow his flight until I could no longer see him. Forcing myself to take slow deep breaths, I drove on.

Walking into the quiet office, I went directly to the young women seated there and told them in a firm, clear voice that I was there to see Daby. Their faces did not change in the slightest. With a small, polite smile, one of them asked me to please have a seat and wait just a moment. I backed up woodenly to a chair, for I dared not take my eyes from their faces. I sat facing them, scrutinizing their eyes, lips, eyebrows, watching their every eye movement and body movement. One turned and started typing into a computer while the other stood behind her, watching the screen. They seemed to stop, to be reading something. Then they turned to me in unison.

"Won't you come on inside to one of the exam rooms?"

As I walked back to the exam room, I knew. The unthinkable had happened.

Dr. McMillan immediately entered the room looking very distressed and said quickly, "It's bad. She's gone."

A child somewhere inside my heart began a soundless scream, a long unwavering wail, and then abruptly stopped as a wide heavy door came sliding down from above, slamming down on it all.

Perhaps I needed a few minutes alone, he said. He left me, gently reassuring me that he would be back shortly.

After a few minutes of staring at a black-framed diploma on the wall, I followed him. "I . . . can't stay in here. What do I need to do?" I asked weakly, numbness filling my body.

"I am so completely puzzled as to the turn of events, Jessica, and I am so, so sorry," Dr. McMillan offered gently. "When I found her dead this morning in her cage, my first thought was of your request to be with her. I really would like to do an autopsy right away, with your permission, to shed some light on this mysterious case."

"Yes. I wish you would," I whispered. *This isn't real, isn't happening,* I kept telling myself.

"I'll try to be as quick as possible. I know that the waiting is difficult. You can wait in one of the exam rooms if you wish."

"No. I'll be outside," I said heavily, and walked outside toward my car. Opening the car door, I sat down on the seat, trying to survive, to deal with the pain. It was so unbearable that it frightened even itself and retreated hastily in shame into the shadows to wait, leaving flaming fragments in its wake.

Then suddenly, Dr. McMillan was at my side, squatting on his heels by the open car door.

"I don't know what to make of this, Jessica, but her lungs were the worst I have ever seen, completely filled with pus and fluid. There was hardly a fraction of breathing space left over in the air sacs. How she lived, breathing normally, for as long as she did absolutely baffles me. I have taken smears of the pus in her lungs and have sent them out to a lab, so we should have the results within a day or two."

Trembling again, I found myself fumbling in my bag for a blue envelope I had tucked into it before leaving the house that morning. Inside it was picture of Baby, Zeke's malamute. I handed it to him and told him the story of Daby's coming.

"Oh, my God," he said softly as he looked for a long time at the picture. Then, motioning for one of his attendants to come to me, he turned and slowly walked away.

The attendant approached me and suggested that I let her drive my car around to the back in order for them to place Daby's body in the car.

"Do you want her in the trunk or the back seat?" she asked softly.

The question seemed ludicrous, bizarre. *The trunk? Of course not! She always rides in the back seat.*

As she drove the car around the building I walked back to the lobby and dialed Patty's number. She answered the ring quickly. For a long moment, I could not speak.

"Hello? Hello?" she repeated, concern creeping into her voice.

"Patty, I am in Gallatin at my old vet's office. Daby is dead. They tell me she is dead. I need you. Don't come here, but please meet me at the house as soon as you can."

"I'll be there right away," she quickly assured me. Her voice sounded faint and very, very far away.

The attendant returned shortly and handed me the car keys. I walked out of the building to the front where they had left my car. Looking toward the back window, dread almost spun me harshly around, sending me running, running forever from the terrible sight of her lifeless body.

I opened the door and knelt down. She lay in the back seat in a bright blue plastic body bag the color of her eyes. I could see the outline of her long nose, and I reached out and caressed it. As I drove the long miles home, I kept my eyes locked on the road before me. As cars passed us by, heedless and speeding to their destinations, I found myself asking, *Can't they tell? Doesn't my car give some sign that it bears an angel?"*

Driving into the garage with her, I saw Max and Maria moving rapidly out of the shadows toward us. As I opened the door, they crowded around me, ears back, looking apologetically at me, then sadly at the blue bag in the back.

I ran upstairs, frantic, my thoughts scrambled. I didn't know what to do next, so I paced from room to room, looking for some sign of her. There was her quilt on the floor by the bed, and her bowl. The phone rang and I yanked it up. It was Carla, who had seen my return from her window.

"Jessica? How is Daby?"

"Daby is dead. I can't talk right now, Carla." I laid the phone down on its cradle.

Then I heard the high, despairing sobs of someone coming up the back stairs. I glanced out the window and saw that it was Carla. I opened the door and she stood before me, a tear-stained child.

"Oh, Jessica! I am so sorry! I feel so responsible."

She looked so grief-stricken and in so much agony that I took her in my arms and found myself comforting her. Then we went down to the garage and lifted the blue bag out of the back seat and onto the hood of the car. I turned and grabbed a pair of grass shears from a shelf and began to cut the bag away.

Daby looked so small, her beautiful coat gone. Over her chest and her back were long, ugly incisions held together by wire sutures. Blood trickled from her mouth.

Zooming backward in time, I am again standing by Zeke, looking down at him as he lay dying, his chest and back covered with large, ugly incisions held together by wire sutures, blood trickling from his mouth.

A car approached, and then a car door quickly slammed. Patty entered the garage, ran to me and held me. We looked down, unbelieving, at Daby's body. It was a hot July day. Flies were humming and buzzing around us.

"We must bury her quickly," I said firmly, grabbing a shovel and handing two others to Patty and Carla. I chose her favorite place directly in the center of the flower garden, and we began to dig. I was trembling violently. Tears and sweat and dirt mingled on my hands and face. A hardness rose up and began to spin strands of steel. I could only faintly hear my heart-child in the faraway distance, behind the heavy door, crying out her unwavering wail. With gritted teeth, I resisted the waves of weakness and nausea and the black spots that were floating past my eyes.

A deep hole finally dug, Patty and Carla rested on a garden bench while I went upstairs for my best white, hand-crocheted lace tablecloth. Then, I sat down to write out a eulogy for her.

Not enough! Not enough! None of this is enough, or is befitting of her, my mind shrieked. A reassuring voice whispered, *But for now, it is all you have.*

We struggled with her heavy body, rolling it gently into the grave where I had placed the tablecloth. Then we folded it around her. That beautiful, precious face . . . I looked at her for one last time, then pulled the lace across it. Turning on soft music, I gasped out her eulogy and we began to fill in her grave. It was blazing hot, and we worked quickly to protect her from the flies.

Carla slipped inside her house to leave Patty and me alone together. We sat for a very long time, not speaking. There was nothing to be said. There was so much to be said. So we sat in silence. It was beginning to grow dark and in the distance, I heard the soft cooing of a mourning dove.

After Patty went home, I set up the CD player on the walkway under the pergola and placed several small candles around her grave. Then I scattered fragrant white rose petals over it. I pushed the long staff of a torch into the ground by her grave and lighted it. Back inside, I gathered all the music that she and I had listened to, had grieved for Zeke by, had played in ecstatic joy for her arrival. I vowed that her candlelight vigil would proceed every night for seven nights, through the night of the seventh day. I sat on the walkway and turned on the music. The music lifted up to the stars. The tall flowers around her grave seemed to bow to her in the flickering candlelight. In the distance, a dog howled. A night bird began to sing.

D r. David called the next day to give me the results of the wound cultures.

"It's just the most incredible thing. She had a very rare organism in those wounds that I, for one, have never run across in my practice. I called four other veterinarians who told me that they haven't seen it either. It is called Flavimonas Habitans. You know, Samantha's mouth was cultured, and it wasn't there. This organism is resistant to all the more common antibiotics.

"This has been such a complicated case, with unexpected twists and turns all over the place. Mysterious.

And I think of the woman who was going to keep her, who brought her here, of all places, where we knew her and knew who she belonged with. Then shortly afterwards, all this began to happen."

We talked at length, and I again told him of my gratitude for his efforts and that I hoped he would continue to watch over Max, Maria, and Peaches. He said that he would.

Dr. McMillan called the next day with news of the smear taken from her lungs. The results indicated "blastomycosis," a condition unrelated to her wound infections, a fungus infection of the lungs that is relatively rare and can be contracted only when conditions are just right. Several factors have to be present at the same time in the environment, and it is most often seen in the autumn, not in July.

He continued, "Blastomycosis can run a long, chronic, smoldering course. But perhaps her system was weakened by the wound infections, so the disease exploded into full bloom. Or perhaps the other way around. I personally believe that she would have died from the blasto even had she not had the infected wounds at all."

After talking with both veterinarians, I leaned back on the sofa and sighed. *Well, Daby, it seems that, knowing you must leave, you had all your bases covered . . . a rare, almost unheard-of organism in those wounds, resistant to most antibiotics, and a fungus infection of the lungs, suddenly bursting into deadly virulence.*

I had taken up residence, day and night, on the sofa, leaving only to feed Max, Maria, and Peaches, eat a little cereal, and return at night to Daby's graveside for her candlelight vigil. I called the hospital and told them that I was ill and would not be in the following weekend. For almost two weeks, I plunged into total darkness, an unfamiliar land. After Zeke's death, I had had Daby, and although the grief had been very intense, I had not visited as dark a place as this. It was very, very dark. There was no light at all, anywhere. I lay on the sofa, seemingly paralyzed.

One night I lay staring into the darkness, for when the sun went down and the light faded, I never bothered to turn on a lamp. But something was pushing at me, nudging, nibbling at my consciousness. *There is something I am supposed to remember. But what?*

I felt heavy and sluggish and dull. In my agony, I thought of how Daby had orchestrated the process of her dying. It was clear that she had decided to spare me the pain of witnessing the moment of her death. Normal lab reports . . . only tiny gasps occasionally in her breathing . . . while her entire lung field was filled with pus and fluid. In her infinite love and wisdom, she knew that my heart could take only so much.

A tiny flame leapt into being as if someone had struck a match in a dark room. Then I remembered the dream. Again, I saw myself preparing to dive into a deep green ocean from a tremendous height. And then the words, "If you struggle you will drown, for the height of the plunge is too great and you will descend deep into the water before returning to the surface."

Once more, the soul's message had been given with stunning clarity. The leap into the deepest depth imaginable was the loss of Daby, a turning point in my soul's path and a challenge to my vision and love to let her go.

And the feminine voice, clear and strong at the end of the dream as I plunged, falling, falling . . . "Remember the Seadog, for she will always be with you. You only have to open the door and she will be there."

Rising from the sofa, I found a dictionary and feverishly flipped through the pages to "Seadog." It read, "a fog bow, an arch of pale, white light, much like a rainbow, opposite the sun."

Leaning my shoulder against the heavy door separating me from my heart-child, I pushed hard, the door swung wide open, and she came running to me. I held her and let the healing sobs and pain come.

That night, I left the sofa and slept in my bedroom, though I tried to avoid looking at Daby's place by my bed. I awakened the next morning to a day of celebration.

Walking into the kitchen to make coffee, I noticed birds flying past the window. It didn't seem odd until I saw that they were everywhere, hundreds of them, of all kinds. The air was thick with them. Walking out onto the deck, into the bright sunlight, I saw that the hickory-nut tree was teeming with them, was alive with them, every limb loaded with birds singing with all their might and strength.

Filled with awe, I walked on around the deck to a spot directly above Daby's grave. Birds were swooping down low from every direction and flying over her grave, perching on the tall flowers growing there, hopping around on the grave itself and along the chainlink fence. Usually shy, they were whirring around my head. In fact, butterflies in dazzling colors seemed to be opening and closing their wings on every single flower. And in addition to birds and butterflies, hummingbirds were everywhere.

It took my breath away. I knew immediately that they were gathering in celebration and in honor of Daby, of her coming and of her return to her purely spiritual form. I ran back inside, put on one of my favorite pieces of music, flung open all the doors, and joined them.

For hours their sweet voices filled the air, and as I stood watching, the feathered celebrants gently took their leave, one at a time, gradually flying away. Only a few remained. And the mourning dove could still be heard in the distance, cooing her soft call.

Returning inside, feeling the celebration of her, the intense joy once again, my gaze fell upon a book lying on the coffee table. It was called *The Souls of Animals,* by Gary Kowalski. I had bought it soon after Daby's arrival. I turned to the publisher's name, for it had occurred to me while watching these beautiful beings honor her, that I must tell Daby's story and share her message. But then, perhaps it was only for me and my family to know. The answer would be revealed. I only had to trust and be open to either possibility.

I picked up a pen and began to write a letter to Stillpoint Publishing.

CHAPTER NINE

MESSENGERS OF HEALING

WHILE I HAD LONGED TO BE ALONE after Zeke's death, I found myself urgently reaching out to others after Daby's departure. Like a vulnerable and needy child, I called Mother and Dorian to "please come, as soon as you can." They came and sat with me as I poured out my anguish and love for Daby, listening quietly and looking lovingly at me with tear-filled eyes. As I allowed myself to need them, I seemed to meet them for the first time, to see them separately from their traditional roles as mother and sister. We were all fellow souls on this journey, I realized, and I felt a level of honor for them that I had never before experienced.

It was perhaps fitting that I was alone with Daby for a week after her departure. Only I and occasionally Carla came to the graveside vigil. None of Daby's neighborhood friends came except for the little child, Elyse, holding tightly to the hand of her father. I could still hear her excited squeals from two houses down, as Daby had romped and played with her daily. She would cry out in delight, "Daby, Daby, Daaaaby!"

That others did not come to say "farewell" deeply saddened me. But somehow, I could feel Daby's comforting thoughts: "Don't be distressed. After all, I was in the form of a dog, and for many people—adults, that is—it may be an embarrassment to honor and pay tribute to this form when it leaves the Earth. Just love them, despite their ignorance."

Patty had said her good-byes at the burial, Sherri was assisting Alvatti in a move to South Carolina and was far away, and Harley called, but set protective boundaries around his own fragile, healing emotions over Zeke's passing. John was embroiled in some kind of attorney thing and could not break away, but called and spoke tender words of affirmation of Daby and of his experience of her and of his love for me.

Max and Maria had begged constantly to be allowed into the house that first week as I lay immobilized on the sofa. After that I let them in, and they covered me with kisses and hovered over me constantly. I experienced tremendous comfort from them with their wistful, "down 'n' outer" eyes.

Max

Maria began to visit Carla to comfort her as well, sometimes spending the night with her beside her bed.

My return to work was made easier by Gini, once again my working partner. She invited me to talk about Daby, about my grief, and about what the entire experience meant to me. She immediately seemed to catch the spirit of it all and affirmed my perceptions and intuitions. In fact, she affirmed me, and we began to form an intimacy and a friendship that we had never known before. I seemed to be truly experiencing her for the first time.

My relationship with Carla, on the other hand, was hanging in a delicate balance. I was passing through the anger stage of grief, finally realizing those feelings after the initial shock and wrenching grief of the first few days. One day, she tremulously asked me if I wanted her to leave. Unable at that time to embrace my need to fully grieve Daby alone, I told her no.

But a little later, as anger and anguish surfaced once again, I accepted my need to ask her to leave. It was not about blame, for Daby's departure had involved many pieces that could have led to wrangling forever about who was guilty of what.

If I had taken her to Dr. David when she first came to my bedroom and refused to leave. . . . If only I had not taken the leash off Samantha that day. . . . If Dr. David had only done that this. . . . If Dr. McMillan had only done that. . . . If Carla had only told me prior to her moving here about Samantha's aggressiveness. . . .

Blaming could go on and on, but my primary anger was with Samantha's violent, aggressive act, so completely alien to Daby and her loving essence. That she should die as a result of violence was an enigma. So it was not about blame. More than anything else, it was to clear the space that I fiercely needed in order to move through my grief over her loss.

The day I asked Carla to leave, my anguish was full-blown. She responded with bewilderment and hurt. I had grown to care for her deeply and felt torn and conflicted by it all. As she prepared to go, I felt an intense sadness for her, knowing how she must feel to be leaving under such circumstances. I wanted to comfort her again and hold her in my arms, but it was not the time or place. I was afraid that if I did so, I would lose my resolve and thus harm us both.

The day Carla left, a friend of hers brought his truck to help her move some of her remaining things. I approached her in the garage.

"Carla, I don't know what to say. I feel confused and very, very sad. I do know that I still care about you and what happens to you. You've sailed through this thing with flying colors, with grace and compassion under the most difficult, awkward, and painful circumstances for me and, at times, for yourself."

She was crying, as was I. Then she flashed that wonderful child-smile and said, "Jessica, I, too, have been confused. I'm not sure what all this is about, but I know it is about something big. I know we're going to learn something from this that will affect our lives forever. And I truly care about you, too."

I watched as the truck went down the drive and onto the street. Maria, ever the comforter, began to run after it. I saw the truck stop out on the street and I saw Carla jump out. Maria ran to her and Carla, kneeling down, embraced her for a long moment, then stepped back into the truck and was gone.

We talked afterwards occasionally, she still wondering why it had been her role to aid in the divine plan for Daby's departure.

"Maybe someday we'll know, huh, Jessica?"

"Yes, Carla, I think we will. But I do know now that only a brave spirit would have been given the task that you received, a spirit that longs for ever-increasing levels of awareness and love, like yours."

It was clear that Samantha had been a part of the plan for Daby's exit from the Earth. But why through violence? Could Daby not have chosen an illness, perhaps just the blastomycosis alone? Or had she, in this way, been presenting another opportunity for our enlightenment?

I had long been interested in the subject of evil. Was it a separate power or the product of humankind's free will? Was it necessary so that we could grasp the nature of good by contrasting it with the nature of evil? Would its elimination also eliminate true freedom of choice? Does light needs darkness to define it?

Bishka and El came from South Carolina for a brief visit in August. As we sat out on the deck in the shadows of late afternoon with the hummingbirds whizzing around our heads, I asked them, "Why the violence?" I was still very angry with Samantha and had fantasies of her being destroyed.

Looking tenderly at me, El said, "There are no direct opposites. They only seem so. This seeming duality can ultimately unify us."

I was reminded of the English poet William Blake, one of my favorites, who had said, "No goods or evils are absolute;

all deities reside in the human breast." True good arises from the balance, union, and integration of the opposites.

For the title page of his work, *The Marriage,* Blake drew an angel and a demon embracing. Reason and emotion, love and hatred, passive and active, good and evil, all must merge into a transcendent, integrated whole.

Carl Jung said that our shadow selves consist of unintegrated elements. If these unconscious elements can be brought to the surface, they can be integrated into a whole. If left repressed, they fester and sap strength. The more the shadow is isolated and repressed, the more violent and destructive it becomes.

And I was reminded of Zeke's words: "If we can only resolve and transcend the conflict within us, we will enter a world of peace. If we yearn for a healing of the world, then the healing must be done within my own heart."

Was this, then, the last message from Daby? That the healing of sickness, violence, and evil can be accomplished only through the power of love? If so, that process will enable the victim to become the victor.

Bishka reflected, "There is a reality that is truly governed by love, Light, and truth. Daby exposed her Light, her truth, her beauty, and her sweetness to all— even to a negative energy, which can block its own Light. Considering who she was, she could have done it no other way."

One afternoon as the sun was setting, I stood on the deck looking out over the water. In that moment, I felt a profound sense of emptiness and loss, both for Zeke and for Daby.

Suddenly, I was startled by a loud, defiant, screeching cry coming from behind me. Directly over me flew a large bird. It practically touched my head as it swooped down from out of the sky. As it flew on in front of me, dropping lower and lower over the yard and the water, I saw that it was the blue heron! She glided down, down across the river, and landed in the shallow water. There she stood, looking directly at me, motionless, elegant. I had seen her this far up the river and close to the house only once before, for she was usually seen only at a distance in the lagoon. Her sudden appearance seemed to say, "You are not alone. We are all around you—not as close by as Daby was, but the time for that has passed."

She stood for a long while, never turning her head from my direction, then lifted up once again and flew back down the river.

From time to time, and usually when I was at a point when I needed a reminder, I would see her standing, alone and lovely, in the lagoon by the park, watching as I drove by.

Once again I searched hungrily for the deeper levels of meaning beneath Daby's coming, sifting through books of all kinds. And once again, the stack of books beside my bed grew tall.

I discovered numerous fascinating beliefs about angels, all of which held some element of truth for me. Some believe that angels can take many forms of disguise, appearing in whatever form the visited person is willing to accept, and never too far removed from natural events. This is perhaps done so that skeptics may easily explain them away and go undisturbed by their presence, if they so choose.

Others believe that angels return to Earth in any form they choose or are assigned. In fact, many religions hold that angels are spiritual beings who were once human, but have evolved into higher forms of celestial wisdom and love. The form they take is the appropriate vehicle to teach or heal those of us still living here on Earth.

Animals have long been regarded as one form in which divine beings have manifested themselves. I'd always known that the ancient Egyptians considered birds the physical and spiritual intermediaries between Heaven and Earth. They saw these winged creatures as representing the flight of the human soul between the living and the dead. The crane and the heron were seen as divine messengers known for their vigilance, longevity, wisdom, and fidelity, their wide wingspans symbolizing their capacity to attain higher levels of spiritual consciousness. The dove and the hummingbird were also considered messengers, the latter a symbol of rebirth, joy, beauty and speed. The owl, as we learn in childhood, is often regarded as a symbol of wisdom and prophecy.

Butterflies have long symbolized the rebirth of the soul, as they make their physical transition from caterpillar to beautiful winged creature.

From my cherished book, *The Souls of Animals*, I read, "Animals, like us, are living souls. They are not things. They are not objects. They dance. They suffer. They know the peaks and chasms of being. Animals are expressions of the Mind-At-Large that suffuses our universe. With us, they share in the gift of consciousness and life."

As I read my books on spiritual animal lore, I recognized things that I had known or read before. But now they felt stunningly powerful, clarifying all that I had sensed and felt as I observed the presence of various creatures both before and after Daby's departure.

I had become more and more aware of their beautiful and wondrous attendance all around me. Now I saw them as true expressions of a tremendous force of intelligence and love that pervades our universe, and could feel God present in all of these creatures.

Propped up in bed one night, reading, I considered the whole subject. Is the animal form "too lowly" for an angel to inhabit? Perhaps man's "dominion" over Nature's creatures does not extend to the spiritual, for are they not in the closest communion with the natural world and thus closer to the divine? Why aren't more incidents reported of divine messengers in physical form?

Perhaps we are not open to their presence. Perhaps they are here, all around us, but we are looking at them through an intellect limited by what our culture teaches us—that the only true reality is a purely physical one. Meanwhile, behind their disguises, these angelic beings challenge our capacity for compassion and reverence and spiritual wisdom.

Obviously, if we were greeted with a tall, glowing figure in a radiant white cloak with huge golden wings, we'd stop cold in our tracks—and, further, we would be on our best behavior! But what about the more humble forms of life? The red bird that frequents the tree outside the window, the yellow cat that suddenly appears on the doorstep, the old man in rags sitting on a park bench. . . .

My thoughts then turned to the mysterious old man in rags, the last person to walk down the aisle at Zeke's funeral. There had been a continuous low murmur among those in the room until he had begun his slow journey down the aisle. It had faded slowly away, and as the old man approached the casket, the room was filled with total silence. Watching him, my scalp had begun to tingle, and my intuition told me that something phenomenal and wondrous was happening. Patty said later, "I restrained myself from running to him to comfort him. There was something otherworldly taking place. It was downright spooky."

As I remembered Daby's persistent efforts to accompany us to the funeral home, I wondered if perhaps she had been there after all. Perhaps we hadn't recognized her in the form she had chosen—that of a ragged old man, another form Zeke had loved.

And perhaps as we move toward the year 2000, we will begin to see and accept guidance that works within nonphysical reality, such as dreams, intuitions, hunches, and sudden inspirations. I know that when we open ourselves to the very real existence of our guides, who appear in various disguises to help us on our journeys, our lives can become richer, fuller, and more authentic. Only then do we reach beyond our normal levels of loving, understanding, and compassion to find new heights, new ways of being in the world.

CHAPTER TEN

DREAMTIME

A ND WHAT OF THE ROLE PLAYED BY DREAMS in this amazing adventure—one that continues to unfold in multiple dimensions? Shortly after Zeke's death, Patty and Alvatti had very vivid dreams of him. They excitedly reported to me that there had been no dream-like quality to their dreams, but rather, a sharp, clear reality, as if he had used the dream state to visit them.

Patty described hers first, saying, "I was standing in a line of people before a platform, and I had the feeling that it was like a train station. There was a door opening onto the platform. Suddenly, Daddy walked through the door onto the platform. I almost exploded with joy and surprise at seeing him. I got out of line, went under the rope and ran to him as he walked rapidly down the platform steps toward me. He was grinning that big grin, his eyes twinkling, alive with love for me. He opened his arms wide and held me close. I could *feel* him, his body, next to mine. I cried, 'Daddy! I thought you were dead!'

"He said, 'Well, I am . . . and I'm not. You see, I had been out of my body a few times before, but I had always managed to get back inside it. But this time, I couldn't . . . my body was too sick.'

"He had a very cheerful air about him and seemed like his old self, laughing a lot and with mischievous eyes, as if to say, 'I know something that you don't.' Then, the dream faded."

Patty continued, "In the next dream, I was seated on a sofa in a room, and the door opened and Daddy walked through. Beaming at me, he seated himself directly in front of me in an armchair. I sat stunned for minute, then ran to him and jumped into his lap the way I used to when I was a small child, seated sideways, one arm around his neck. 'Daddy! I can't believe you're here!' I cried.

"He smiled tenderly, eyes twinkling as usual, and said, 'Now, you know that what you are seeing is not what I really look like now. I have a new body. What you are seeing is what you were familiar with on Earth.' And then the dream was over.

"In the third dream, he came to me, and again I had the knowledge that he was supposed to be dead, yet was here with me. He was accompanied by a man who stayed in the background, waiting.

"Daddy said, 'Now I must tell you that I am no longer a man.'

"For the first time, I began to argue with him, insisting that he was, indeed, a man and not a woman.

"He replied, 'Oh, no, you don't understand. I am neither a man nor a woman. I have no gender here.' That was the end of the dream."

Patty explained that all her dreams were consistent with the quality of their relationship—loving and honoring of the other, tinged with a sparring kind of camaraderie, as in, "Now, let me tell you about *my* latest discovery!"

Then it was Alvatti's turn. She told me, "During Dad's recovery, he always encouraged me to find the freedom that can only be found within. I resisted for a long time, but slowly my healing began. Then I had a dream after Dad died that showed me what I needed to see.

"Dad walked up to me in the dream and I knew that he wanted me to fly. I leapt into the air, a frantic jump, and landed on top of a small building. Dad was still with me. I stretched out my arms and we looked at each other and lifted up from the building. Then we were flying in the night sky, through the tearing wind, past the stars, together. He said to me as we flew, 'You may think that your flying is a gift from me, but it is your gift to yourself. You have always known how to fly. You only had to remember.'

"Suddenly, he was gone, but still with me in thought, and I was flying over something like a baseball field. It was surrounded by bright lights, with vivid colors glowing from it, reaching high up into the sky. The stands were filled with people. I began to fly around the bases, laughing. It was so much fun! As I did that, the crowd in the stands stood and applauded. The sound was deafening, it was so loud and joyful.

"Then I was flying down into a valley, over another baseball field. It was dark, neglected, unkempt, littered with garbage. I landed on my feet and looked around. I wanted to fly away from there, but suddenly I couldn't. My children, Matthew and Patrick, walked up to me carrying a yellow stick. Seeing the stick, I said, 'That's it! The yellow stick can make me fly again.' But something within me told me that I did not need anything outside of myself to fly, that I had all that I needed within me.

"It was then that I looked into the dark woods surrounding the field and saw a wolf standing at an entrance to a cavern, watching me. It looked hungry, scared, angry and sad. I tossed it the rest of my half-eaten sandwich. The wolf looked at me gratefully.

"Then I turned, my steps buoyant, and I lifted up once again, flying freely in the night sky.

"So, once again," Alvatti pointed out, "I was shown by Dad, my higher self and my Higher Power that I can own my own power and allow myself healing and transformation at the deepest level, where my angry, hungry, hurt, and sad child-within lives. The wolf was my wounded child shadow-self. But when I allow my wounded child this healing, my wonder child, my magical child can come forth.

"Watching Dad as he recovered from alcoholism and seeing the two of you together, I came to know that the more I learned to love and honor myself, the more I would be attracted to people who love and take care of themselves and can love and honor me.

"I saw Dad learn to love himself, and then to love you. You had a good life together and I want that for myself. I will no longer settle for a lesser quality of love, a mutual-dependency thing. I am grateful that I am learning this while I'm young and won't have to wait as long as Dad did, though he was fortunate, indeed, to have learned it."

Shortly after our conversation, Alvatti, who had always lived very close to her mother and sisters, was offered a management position with her company several states away. She saw that the universe and her Higher Power were offering her another opportunity to "fly" in yet another area of her life. So, casting aside her old fears, she accepted. She is still flying.

John and Zeke had frequently teased each other about their weight. One night, Zeke walked briskly up to John in a dream, looking much younger and very trim. He stood before John, smiling broadly. "Can you guess how much I weigh now, John?" he chuckled, eyes dancing.

While John stood astonished and speechless in the dream, Zeke folded his arms across his chest and rocked back on his heels. "I weigh zero! I have no weight!"

Then he moved closer and gave John one of his big warm bear hugs, as he used to do, and John awakened, his face wet with tears.

Estel, Zeke's former wife, also met with him in a dream. All the children sat in chairs behind them. He stood before her with blood on his shirt, over his chest.

"Can I hug you?" she whispered. But it was not with the spoken word that they communicated, but through thought. She felt very peaceful in his presence.

He responded, "Yes, you can touch me and I will feel real to you."

She moved toward him and they embraced. She could feel his body, his touch.

"Do you know that I love you and that I wish we could have been more successful in our life together?" she asked.

He looked at her warmly, sadly. "I know that, and it's all right. It's as it should be."

"Will you come to me again?" Estel asked.

Zeke answered, as he began to fade from her vision, "I'll try, but it's very difficult." Then he was gone.

Sherri experienced his presence one day shortly after his death as she was lying on his bed, sleeping.

"It was like a dream and it wasn't like a dream. I was in deep despair. Then I felt his Earth form, his body, beside me, cradling me. I could feel his touch and his warmth. He was crooning a lullaby without words, and peace swept over me. I knew that it was a gift he had brought me."

Zeke's children and I continued to talk about our experiences of his passing from this Earth plane and of Daby's coming. They, too, were experiencing deep insights and feeling enriched by the legacy of love and healing left by these two special beings.

As his children continue to grow, I know that wherever he is, Zeke is ecstatic. Always a loving father, I suspect that if he could have selected only one sentence from his eulogy, he would have chosen this one: "He had children who loved him."

My thoughts often returned to those three hours in the intensive care unit as he lay dying, surrounded by his beloved children. While he was dying, Patty, standing at his feet, suddenly called out, "Oh, Daddy!" I'm so excited for you! You're going on an incredible, spectacular journey!"

Amazed by the genuine joy in her voice, I looked at her. Hers was a child's face, radiant and glowing. Perhaps she was remembering what it was like in the next world, her soul's memory breaking through her grief.

Later she said of the outburst, "I had never had that feeling about death before, that wild joy and excitement, like going to Disneyland! I startled myself with it. And it remains with me. I will never fear death for myself or others again. I'll just feel the sadness of missing my loved ones."

The chaplain, a woman who remained with us that last hour with Zeke, said, "This is the most beautiful thing I have ever seen a family do—encircling him, touching each other and him, sending him on his journey, and accepting his need to go with total love."

Patty spoke to me often of her resolve "to stop taking people for granted, as if they will be on Earth with me forever and I have all the time that I need with them. I believe now, as Dad did, that this whole experience on Earth is about love and relationships and how we treat our fellow human beings." She added, "Daby's coming that day changed *everything*. She made Dad's passing more bearable and gave me tremendous hope and comfort."

Sherri said, "One day as Dad and I stood on the deck, talking about my struggle for spiritual growth, he told me, 'You are not a human trying to become spiritual. You are a spirit learning to be human.' I understand what he was telling me. My life here is a choice, a desire to learn. Where better to teach a soul—which is love, understanding, Light and intelligence—about pure love, which is forgiveness of self and others? It's in human form that we feel pain, anger, greed, pride, and jealousy."

She continued, "You know, after you told me, Jessica, about Dad's asking his Higher Power daily to help him avoid hitting any little creatures running across the road, I began to do the same, and it works! I haven't hit a single one since."

Harley opened the floodgates occasionally, calling me and brimming over with feeling, words tumbling over each other.

"I am understanding more about forgiveness through all of this with Dad's leaving. And I am becoming aware of a need to share it with others who may be struggling with the resentment of a parent and with the pain of a childhood's losses. I see now that forgiveness is more of a journey, a process, than a destination. It keeps teaching me all kinds of things as I go along, especially about forgiving myself. Most of all, it has affected and changed, in many ways, my relationship with my children. I hope that I am more fully present with them than before."

His ten-year-old daughter, Jessica, wrote me a letter about her "Grand-Dad, Z."

"Grand-Dad was my best friend. When I was down, he picked me up. Whenever he was down, I picked him up. He gave me things I had always wanted, even though I never told him I wanted those things. But he is not around any more for me to share my secret thoughts with evermore.

But every night I get on my knees and tell him my secret thoughts. One time he took me to a place where his Daddy and him used to go and he took me there and if I have kids I will take them there, too. Because I loved that person and always will. So whenever I am down, he can't really pick me up, but I can always picture it in my heart.

But the funny thing was, he never really died, because every now and then I look at his lucky elephant shirt and I can still see him there, looking in my eyes and waving to me. Your the best ever. But I can't wait until I'm right up there with him giving him a great big hug and from there on out I will never leave his side again. I love you, and I'll always be your pal. Thanks for the good times.

Your granddaughter,
Jessica

John expressed his feelings mostly in his poetry. Having a highly developed social conscience, he shared Zeke's love for the social outcasts, the alienated, the homeless and dispossessed. He wrote a poem about them, dedicating it to Zeke.

BAILEY AVENUE

Just an average apparition
slid to twilight's floor.
a Reaganomics gypsy
and a free-willed garbage-bag-cart
set in motion.
An archangel in tatters
does not choke on puke
and fall
crowned King of nothing
on bailey avenue.

Lifeless pupils betray
the passive surprise
of murderous circumstance
and reflect
a truly gorgeous evening.

Zeke had said of John once, "Oh, that he would only know how wonderful he is and what he is here to do! He is a spiritual warrior and will be, in some way, on the cutting edge of a new world order."

My mother shared with me her thoughts of Zeke and of Daby. "I think Daby was an angel. If anyone could have pulled that one off, Zeke could have!"

A tiny, spunky woman, now in her eighties, she had loved him fiercely. She had never had any man in the family treat her with the honor and cherishing adoration that Zeke did. He told me once that she "felt to me like my grandmother, who was my lifeline until I was around eight years old." He loved our visits with her at her home, would get excited and childlike in his anticipation of going there, feeling warm and safe there. He took her fishing with him, setting up her chair on the bank, fussing over her, making her comfortable, teasing her.

She was devastated by his departure. Usually stoic and tearless, she had sobbed for hours at the news of his death. "I learned so much from him," she told us through her tears.

One young woman sought me out several weeks after his departure. "I was working the switchboard at the treatment center the night of his death. The switchboard became completely jammed with constant calls from former patients, who, having heard the news, were calling in despair to see if it were really true. Then the next day, I went to a gathering of people who had met as a support group. I have never seen so many grown men cry in one place, at one time."

The story of loss and renewal is as old as time itself, I suppose, but somehow, it is created anew, as if for the first time, with each personal loss of someone whom we deeply love. It becomes shatteringly real and we are stunned that it really does happen and that this leavetaking is so final. But death teaches us, breaks us open, lifts, however temporarily, the veil of Earth-dulled illusion. No deeper lessons can be learned, for it is here that we reach, if we are willing and find the courage, for the heart of life to meet our innermost selves.

For are we not all angels, born into a forgetting, now here in a supreme act of courage to realize our highest selves? Is it not here that we connect fully and completely with the Divine, while still in our fragile and doomed physical bodies?

It was in October, after Daby's departure in July, that the news came to me that Ben, my former husband and John's father, had died from a ruptured cerebral aneurysm. He was an active man, an attorney, only fifty-three years old. As he had slept one night, the red explosion in his brain swept him, in his casual, easy Earth-sleep, into eternity. He was comatose for four days and then pronounced brain-dead. John gave permission for his father's heart and kidneys to go to others in need.

I was deeply moved by this gift of life for three people. John did not hesitate in his decision and spoke of it casually, as if it were a perfectly natural thing to do. He told me that the last night he was at his father's bedside, he had felt Zeke's overwhelming and powerful presence in the room.

Ben had been my first love and husband, and he had become a friend in the distance. We had been together in a time and space of ignorance, illusion, and struggle, never really knowing each other or connecting at a deep, intimate level. Our encounters over the last twenty years had been infrequent and, though friendly, had been superficial. Deeply shocked and saddened by his death, I realized there were things I had wanted to say to him, erroneously believing there would be time to meet him, know him truly for the first time. But it was too late.

Then I dreamed I was walking down a hallway in a large, beautiful, white-columned house. The colors were soft light greens, pinks, and violets. I came to a doorway leading into a large bedroom, light streaming in through its many windows. On the bed, Ben lay sleeping. I walked over to the bedside, looking down at him in amazement. He opened his eyes, looked up at me, and smiled.

I exclaimed, "You're supposed to be dead!"

Sitting up slowly up now and swinging his legs over the side of the bed, he said, still smiling, "Oh, really?"

Talking rapidly and excitedly, I began to tell him in a torrent, a rush of words, all that I had wanted to say to him.

He stood, listened quietly, then took both my hands and kissed me lightly on the cheek.

"Thank you," he said softly. He had an air of dreamy peace and calm.

"But what about this problem of everyone thinking that you are dead, and what about your law practice and all your business affairs? Shouldn't you let people know?" I asked, in some agitation.

He seemed slightly embarrassed that I would have such concerns.

"It isn't important," he said. "But there is one thing I ask you to do right away. *Tell John that I still live.*"

And with that he led me out into the hallway where beautiful people were moving excitedly about, preparing a great feast, a celebration.

I awakened abruptly, torn away from the dream by the loud beep of the alarm clock. I distinctly had the feeling of having been with Ben and felt very sad. Yet I was also relieved, elated that I had been given the opportunity to finally tell him what was in my heart.

Following his instructions, I immediately began to write John a letter, for a portion of my grief over Ben's departure was because John had lost his birth father. Zeke had become a father-figure to him, and he and John had been well on their way to an intimacy that is rare between two men, when Zeke left the Earth.

Now, suddenly, Ben had also flown away.

Afterword

AT TWILIGHT, WALKING ON THE LAWN BY THE WATER and the flower garden, I'll sometimes catch a flash of white and gray at the corner of my eye. Then I'll remember, once again, the clear, beautiful voice in the dream: "Remember the Seadog, for she will always be with you. You only have to open the door and she will be there."

And I know that "the door" means my heart and my openness to the utter wonder and magic of this world, both physical and nonphysical. The blue heron reminds me of a continuing loving presence, one that holds within it Daby, Zeke, Ben, and my father, as well as all other loving spirits passing through this Earth plane. The purple and yellow pansies growing on Daby's grave beautify my world, as do the occasional swarms of songbirds and butterflies and the river itself, murmuring softly, rippling green, and at night, shining dark blue under a smiling moon.

I now feel that I am in an enchanted world where there is so very much more than first meets the eye. There are no coincidences.

Death will come to our loved ones and, indeed, to us. We can only embrace the pain in order to heal, and the universe stands ready to aid us in this journey if we but open ourselves. And this, perhaps, is the deepest mystery of all—how life comes forth from death. Not only life, but joy, for there is an interconnectedness in all beings, plants and creatures, and the Earth herself croons to us, nurtures us, and renews us when we allow it.

I believe that Daby was an angel, taking a physical form that my husband loved very much, that of his own beloved Baby. Daby was a messenger, and the message—as my human mind perceives it—is that life after death is very real, is a parallel reality. At times, when the need and the love are great, the veil between worlds shifts, and angels and messages come through in many different forms. Daby was both the messenger and the message, but she had other messages as well—about holding lightly and not clutching, about letting go with love, about patience and humility and quiet dignity. And most of all, she taught me about joy, as I watched her drop her regal bearing to romp and scuffle with Max and Maria, the two "down 'n' outers" that she summoned here to remain with me after her departure. I watched her unfailing joy in others as she made her neighborhood rounds daily, visiting the child, Elyse, the elderly man, and always, daily, trotting off to the park down the street to see the children.

I had always been flooded with an inexplicable joy each time I'd seen her. She might be racing across the lawn, trotting across the deck, lying in her favorite spot in the yard with front paws crossed and head up, or standing at the French doors, her head down, peering inside. I had always been an animal lover, but I had never had feelings like those. They made me think of a phrase that I had heard—"an unbearable lightness of being."

During the last week of her life, as I carried her up and down the deck stairs, I came to know that I would have done anything to make her comfortable, to keep her alive, or to give her whatever she needed from me. There was no holding back. Perhaps that was one of her greatest gifts to me.

And now, as I leave you with my story, I have but one wish.

> *"Unless you become as a little child,*
> *you cannot enter into*
> *the Kingdom of Heaven."*
> *(Matthew 18:2)*

The Kingdom of Heaven is a place of magic, an enchanted forest where colors are breathtaking in their brilliance, and there is holiness and sacredness in all plants and creatures. They can be seen everywhere, in all their exquisite splendor when we are our whole selves, childlike, open, reverent, spontaneous, imaginative, and free. It is truly a place of the heart. Would that we could "roll the stone" back from the heart's door, so that we may remember who we are and why we are traveling here.

My wish is that, from time to time,
we will *all* remember.

ABOUT THE AUTHOR

JESSICA EZELL STILL LIVES IN RURAL TENNESSEE, in the cottage by the river, with Max, Maria, and Peaches, and she continues to work as a Registered Nurse in a unit that treats alcoholism and drug addiction.

From time to time, the blue heron can still be seen standing, elegant and watchful, in the lagoon by the park. And white hyacinths are blooming on Daby's grave.

A portion of the author's proceeds from this book will be contributed to the Tennessee Wildlife Resources Agency and the Alcohol and Drug Council of Middle Tennessee.